Francis Frith's 50 CLASSICS

CATHEDRALS

The Francis Frith Collection

THE FRANCIS FRITH COLLECTION®

First published in the United Kingdom in 2006 by
The Francis Frith Collection

ISBN 1-84589-084-1

British Library Cataloguing in Publication Data

Francis Frith's 50 Classics - Cathedrals
Compiled by Terence and Eliza Sackett

The Francis Frith Collection
Frith's Barn, Teffont,
Salisbury, Wiltshire SP3 5QP
Tel: +44 (0) 1722 716 376
Email: info@francisfrith.co.uk
www.francisfrith.co.uk

Printed and bound in India

Front Cover: **DURHAM**, *The Cathedral from the River 1921* 70712t
The colour-tinting is for illustrative purposes only, and is not intended to be historically accurate

AS WITH ANY HISTORICAL DATABASE THE FRITH ARCHIVE IS CONSTANTLY BEING CORRECTED AND IMPROVED AND THE PUBLISHERS WOULD WELCOME INFORMATION ON OMISSIONS OR INACCURACIES

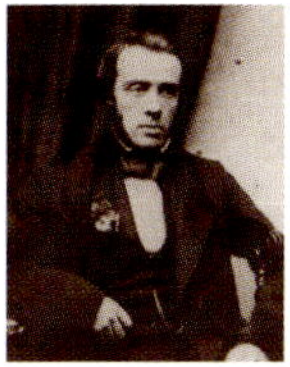

FRANCIS FRITH

VICTORIAN PIONEER

Francis Frith, founder of the world-famous photographic archive, was a complex and multi-talented man. A devout Quaker and a highly successful Victorian businessman, he was philosophic by nature and pioneering in outlook. By 1855 he had already established a wholesale grocery business in Liverpool, and sold it for the astonishing sum of £200,000, which is the equivalent today of over £15,000,000. Now in his thirties, and captivated by the new science of photography, Frith set out on a series of pioneering journeys up the Nile and to the Near East.

INTRIGUE AND EXPLORATION

He was the first photographer to venture beyond the sixth cataract of the Nile. Africa was still the mysterious 'Dark Continent', and Stanley and Livingstone's historic meeting was a decade into the future. The conditions for picture taking confound belief. He laboured for hours in his wicker dark-room in the sweltering heat of the desert, while the volatile chemicals fizzed dangerously in their trays. Back in London he exhibited his photographs and was 'rapturously cheered' by members of the Royal Society. His reputation as a photographer was made overnight.

VENTURE OF A LIFE-TIME

By the 1870s the railways had threaded their way across the country, and Bank Holidays and half-day Saturdays had been made obligatory by Act of Parliament. All of a sudden the working man and his family were able to enjoy days out, take holidays, and see a little more of the world.

With typical business acumen, Francis Frith foresaw that these new tourists would enjoy having souvenirs to commemorate their days out. For the next thirty years he travelled the country by train and by pony and trap, producing fine photographs of seaside resorts and beauty spots that were keenly bought by millions of Victorians.

These prints were painstakingly pasted into family albums and pored over during the dark nights of winter, rekindling precious memories of summer excursions. Frith's studio was soon supplying retail shops all over the country, and by 1890 F Frith & Co had become the greatest specialist photographic publishing company in the world, with over 2,000 sales outlets, and pioneered the picture postcard.

FRANCIS FRITH'S LEGACY

Francis Frith had died in 1898 at his villa in Cannes, his great project still growing. The archive he created continued in business for another seventy years. By 1970 it contained over a third of a million pictures showing 7,000 British towns and villages.

Frith's legacy to us today is of immense significance and value, for the magnificent archive of evocative photographs he created provides a unique record of change in the cities, towns and villages throughout Britain over a century and more. Frith and his fellow studio photographers revisited locations many times down the years to update their views, compiling for us an enthralling and colourful pageant of British life and character.

We are fortunate that Frith was dedicated to recording the minutiae of everyday life. For it is this sheer wealth of visual data, the painstaking chronicle of changes in dress, transport, street layouts, buildings, housing, engineering and landscape that captivates us so much today, offering us a powerful link with the past and with the lives of our ancestors.

Computers have now made it possible for Frith's many thousands of images to be accessed almost instantly. The archive offers every one of us an opportunity to examine the places where we and our families have lived and worked down the years. Its images, depicting our shared past, are now bringing pleasure and enlightenment to millions around the world a century and more after his death.

INTRODUCTION

This colourful pocket book contains 50 classic Frith photographs of English cathedrals.

We see these ancient buildings in their full glory. Some are pictured imposingly sited on hilltops, and others in tranquil riverside settings, their spires and towers rising majestically over the rooftops. There are exterior prospects of magnificent elevations, rich in decoration and carving, and vistas of exquisite interiors—arcades, vaults, chancels and choirs, traceried windows, crypts, aisles, cloisters, gateways, as well as a chained library. Each of the photographs is accompanied by an informative caption.

Evocative and atmospheric, these stunning images will carry you back to a long-vanished era, when the ecclesiastical craftsman's art was at its finest and most impressive.

BRISTOL, THE CATHEDRAL 1887 20141

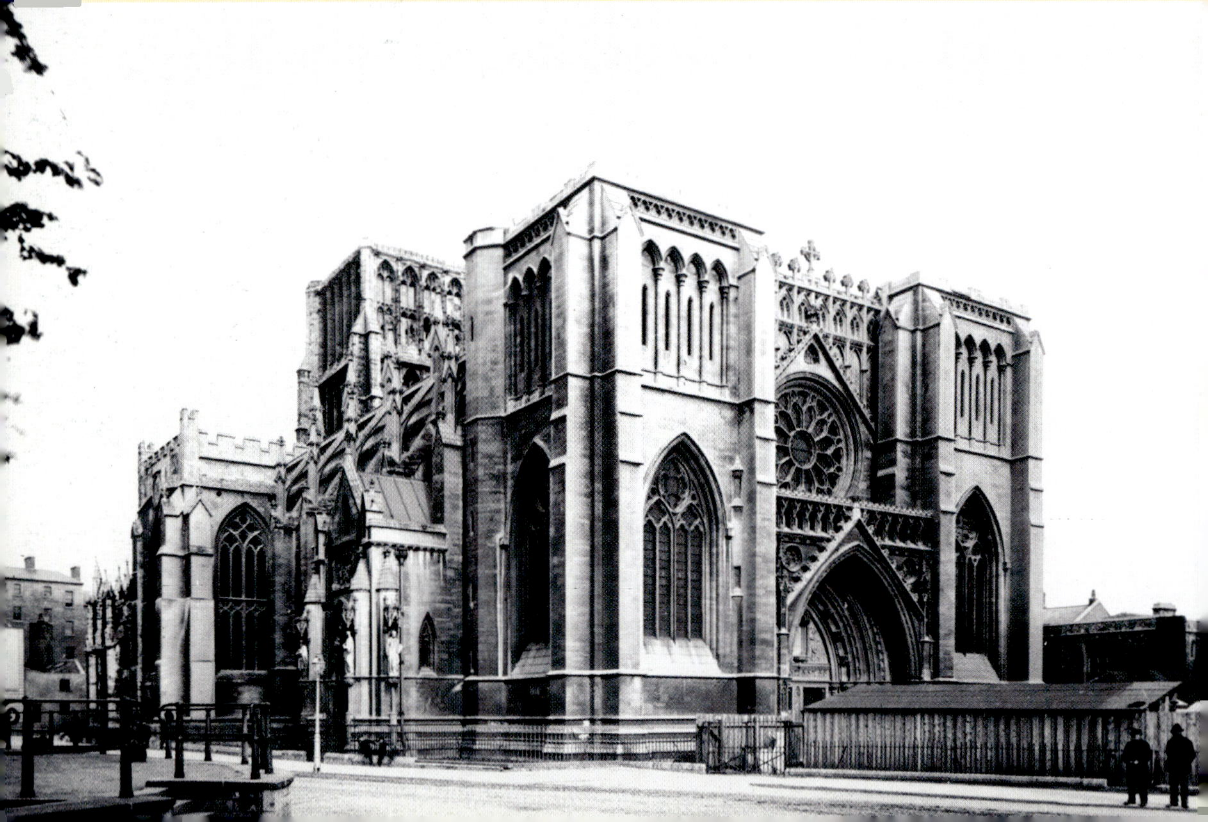

The Bristol diocese was created by Henry VIII in 1542, and comprised eighteen parishes within the city boundaries, fourteen others in Gloucestershire and Abbots Leigh in Somerset. It was refounded by Pope Paul IV in 1557.

Because it lacks a clerestory and triforium, the aisles rise to the same height as the nave, a feature making Bristol unique among English cathedrals. The original Norman nave was partially reconstructed at the time of the Dissolution, but then was allowed to fall into ruin. The present nave is 19th-century, and was built, along with the west towers, between 1868 and 1888.

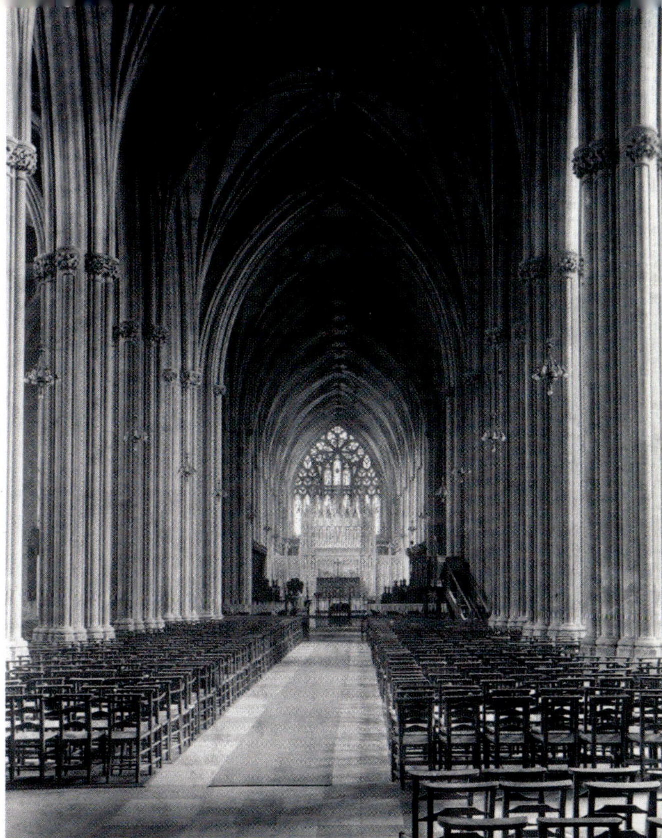

BRISTOL, THE CATHEDRAL, THE NAVE EAST 1900 45572

CANTERBURY, THE CATHEDRAL 1888 21350

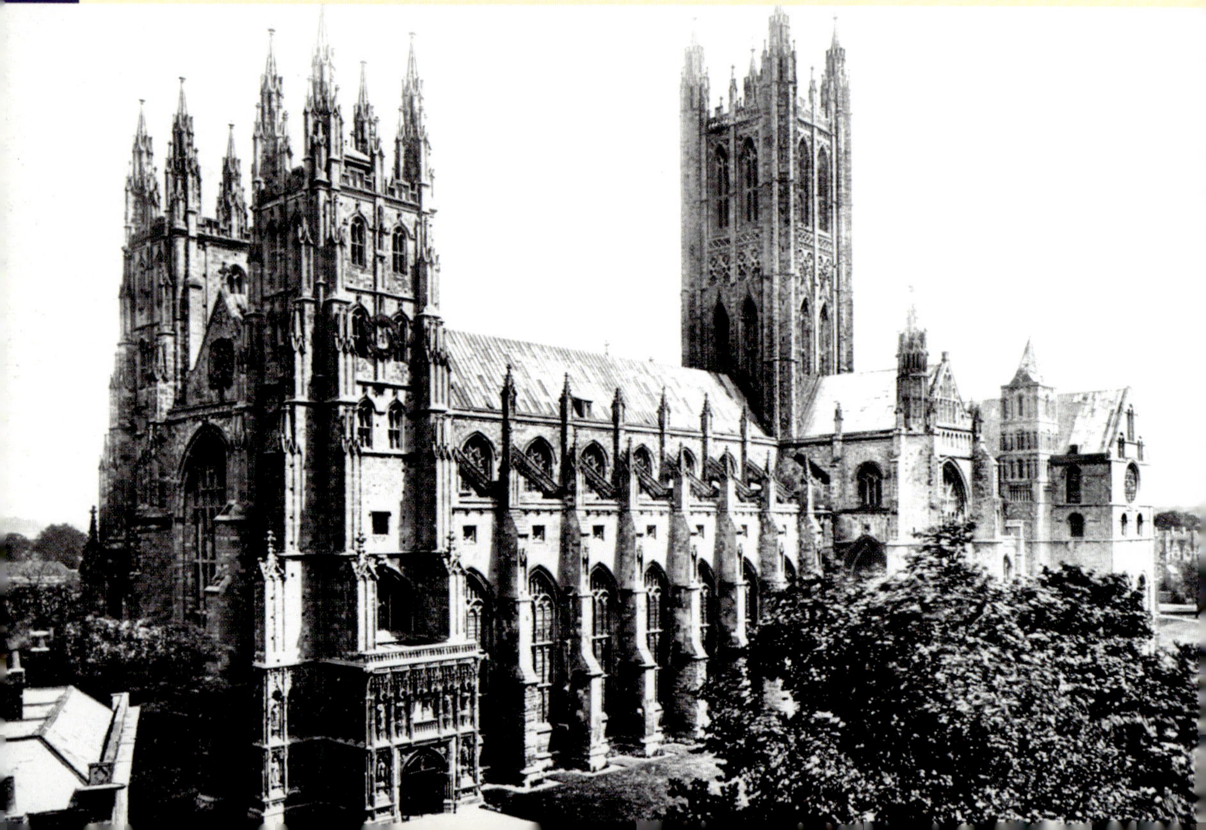

◄ *Since Saxon times, Canterbury has been the spiritual capital of England. The cathedral was rebuilt in the 12th century, when it began to assume the form in which we see it today. It was here that Thomas à Becket was murdered in 1170, and the city has been a place of pilgrimage ever since. In this fine study, the huge west front dominates the scene.*

► *After a disastrous fire in 1174, the new choir was designed by William of Sens, a French master mason who was versed in the Gothic style of northern France, with its pointed arches and universal stone-built ribbed vaults. Canterbury's immense prestige meant that the style chosen became the English norm; it sounded the death-knell of the already declining Anglo-Norman style. William fell from the scaffolding, and his mighty work was completed by William the Englishman.*

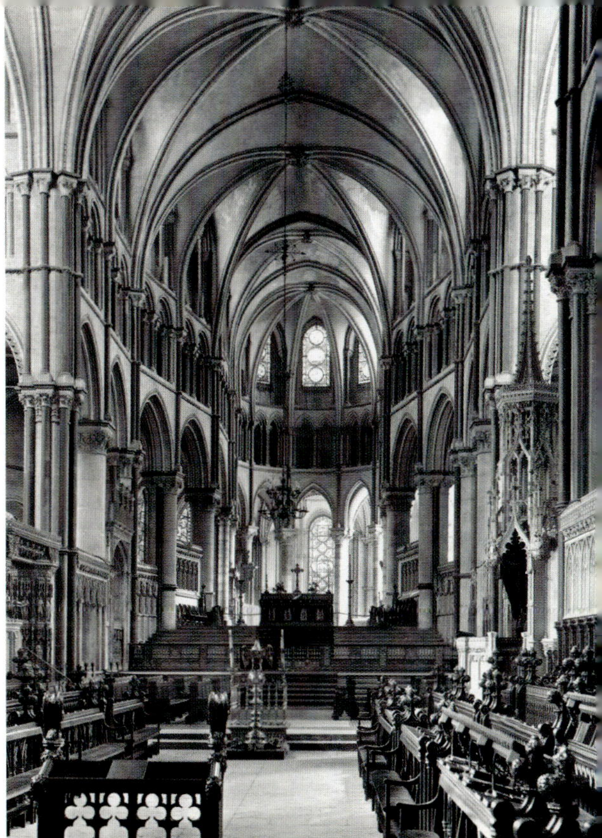

CANTERBURY, THE CATHEDRAL, THE CHOIR, LOOKING EAST 1921 70340

5 **CANTERBURY, THE CATHEDRAL, THE NORMAN CRYPT** 1888 21396

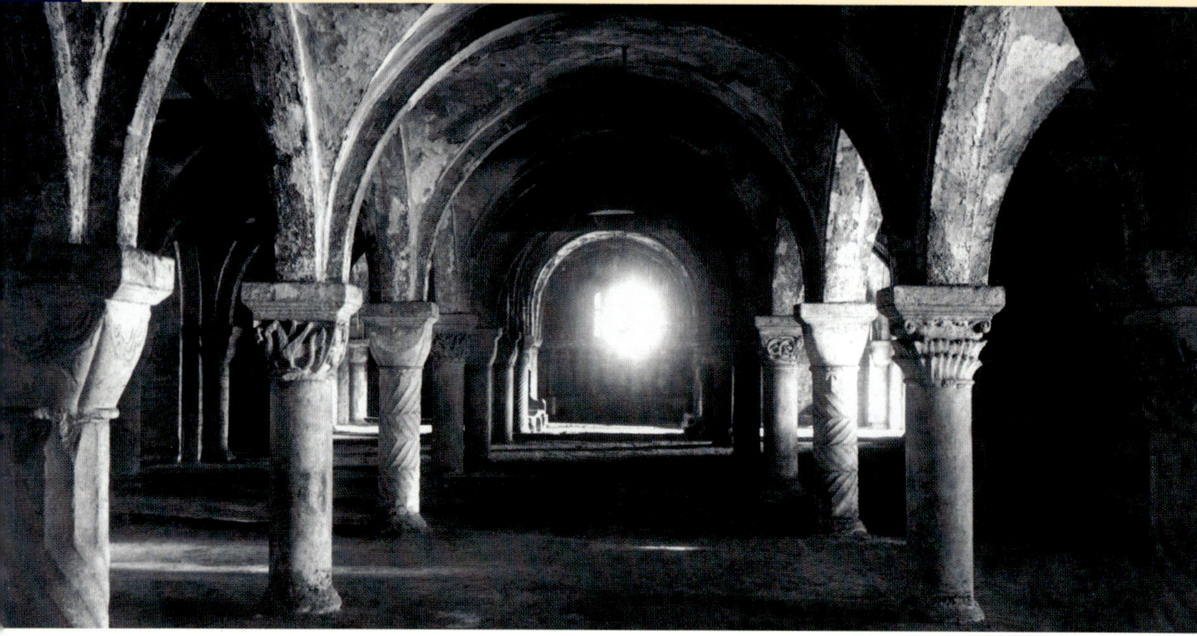

The crypt dates from Norman times, and it is considered to be one of the finest in the world. Note the decorative carving on the pillars, which is similar to that at Durham Cathedral. This atmospheric early photograph emphasises the awesome majesty and ancient mysteries of the Christian tradition.

Built of red sandstone, Chester Cathedral was founded in 1092 as a Benedictine abbey. Parts of the original Norman church can still be seen, though much of the present cathedral dates from the 13th to the 16th centuries. In this photograph, the road appears to sweep straight into the west door. A cab driver and his horse wait patiently in the shade for their next fare.

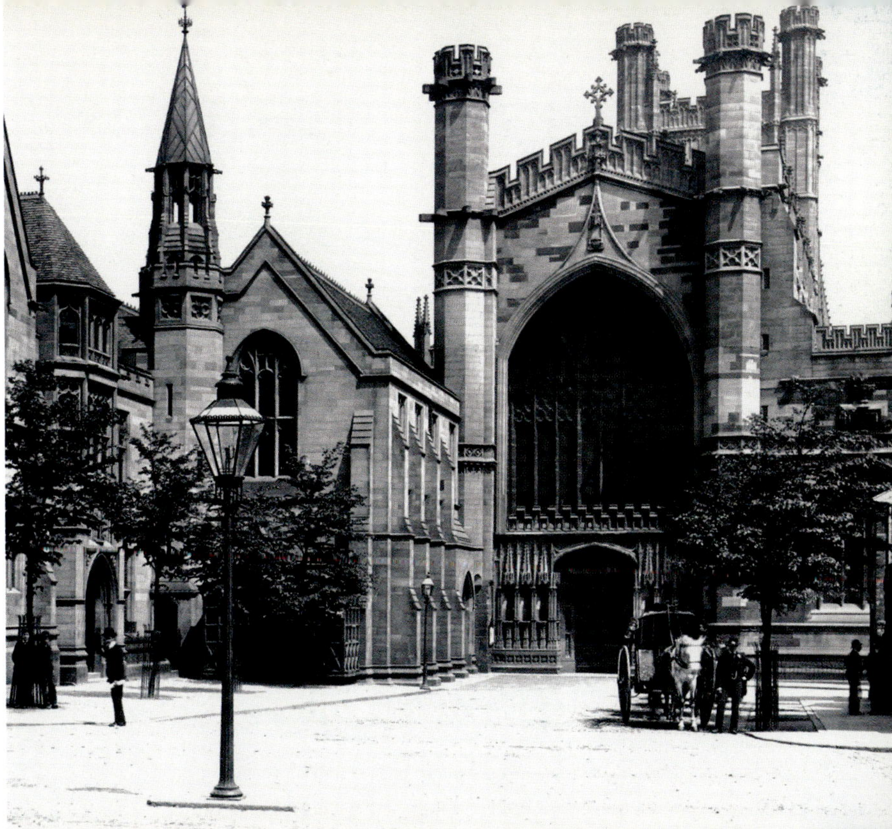

CHESTER, THE CATHEDRAL, THE WEST FRONT 1888 20577

CHESTER, THE CATHEDRAL, THE CHOIR WEST 1888 20583

Intricately carved stalls enclose the choir in a rich setting. The superb wood carving dates from 1380, and on the misericords it depicts vivid scenes of medieval life and legend. A careful restoration programme of the cathedral was undertaken by Sir George Gilbert Scott, the eminent Victorian architect; here in the sanctuary he placed a suspended ironwork cross, which has since been removed.

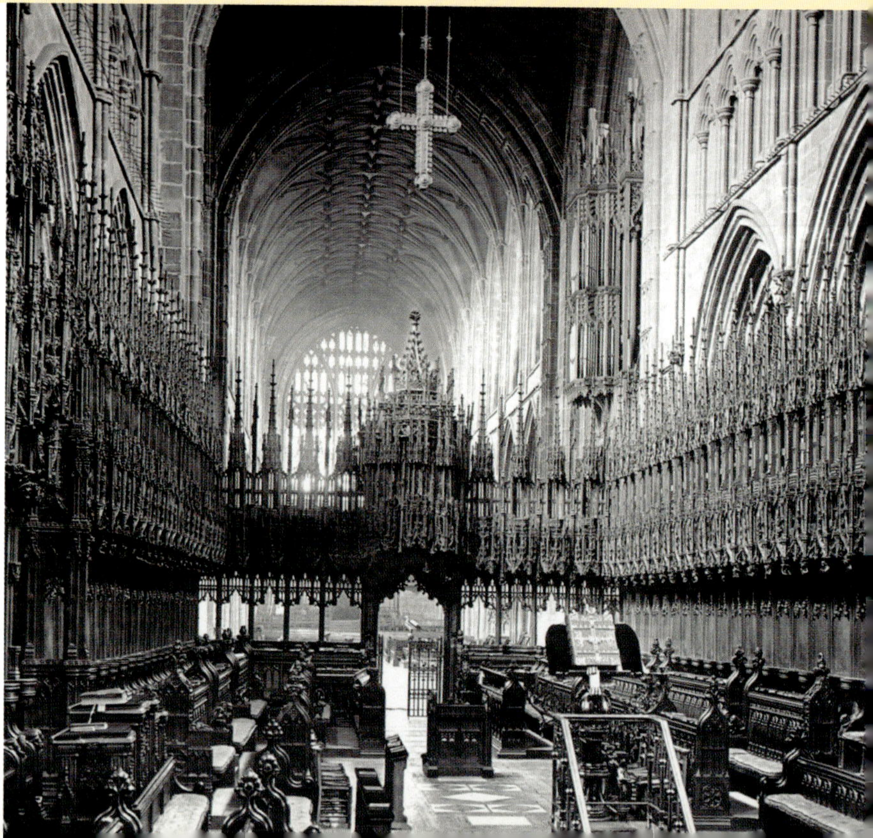

This view is one not normally seen by the public, for it was taken in the Prebendal School grounds. It shows the cathedral's twin west towers: the south one was partially rebuilt in the early 13th century after a storm in 1210, and the other was rebuilt in 1900 after being ruinous since collapsing in 1636. To the left is the detached bell tower.

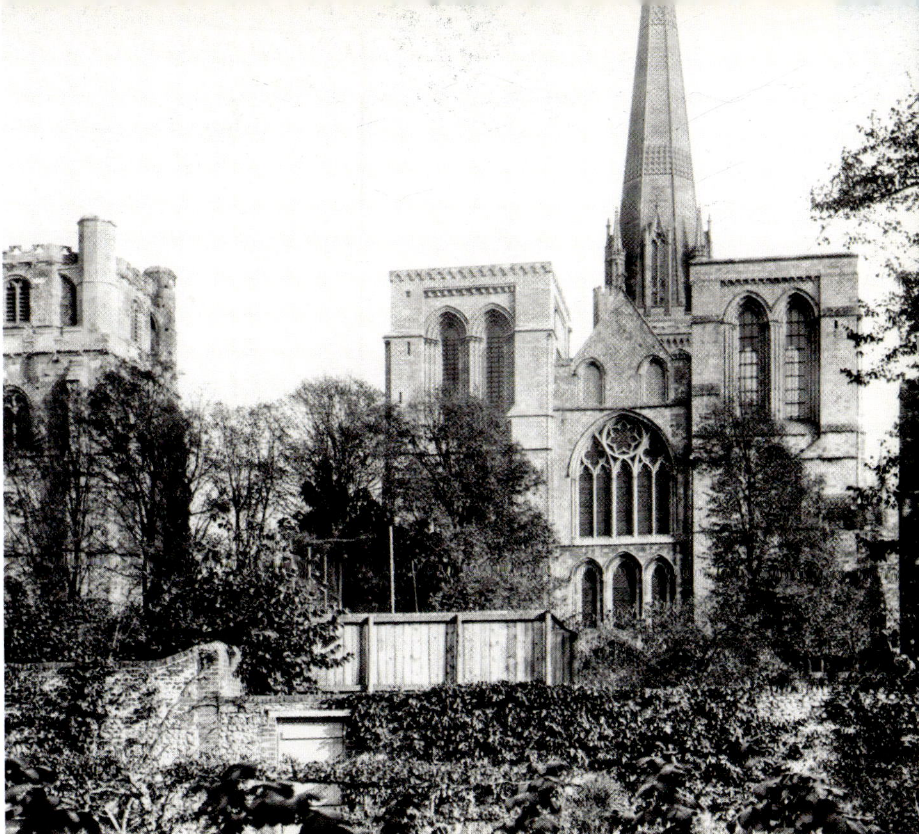

CHICHESTER, THE CATHEDRAL, THE WEST FRONT 1906 55029

Despite having a three-sided cloister, Chichester Cathedral was not a monastic foundation, so the cloisters serve to enclose a tranquil grassy area known as The Paradise. St Richard, whose brightly painted statue is in the niche above the double arch, was Bishop from 1245 to 1253; he was canonised by the Pope in 1262.

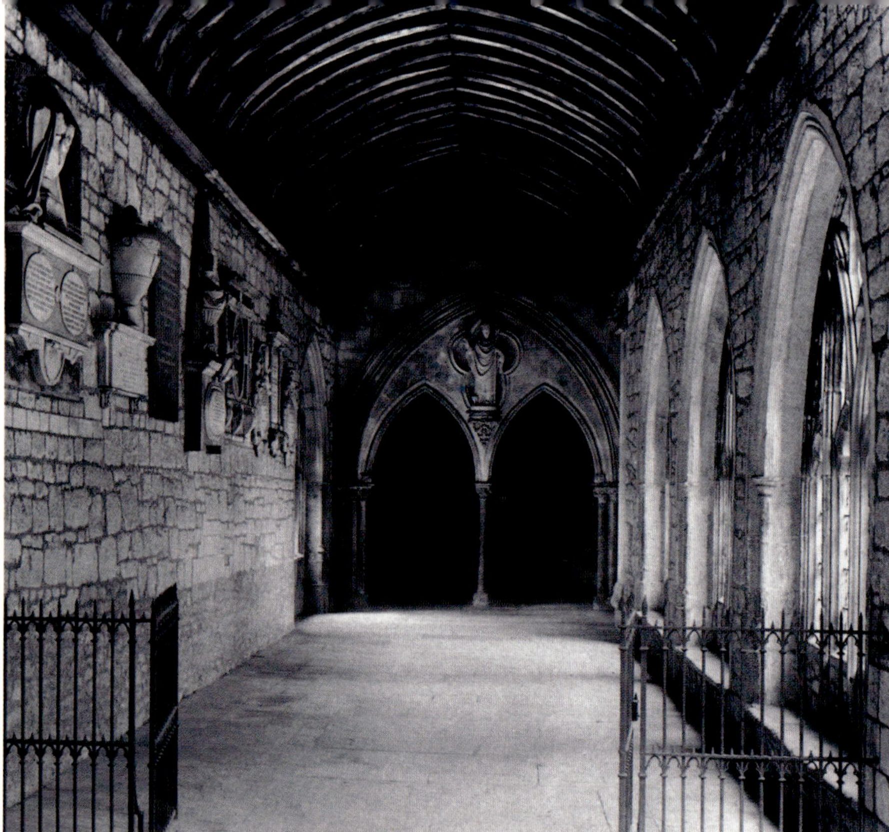

CHICHESTER, THE CATHEDRAL CLOISTERS AND ST RICHARD'S PORCH

1892 29995

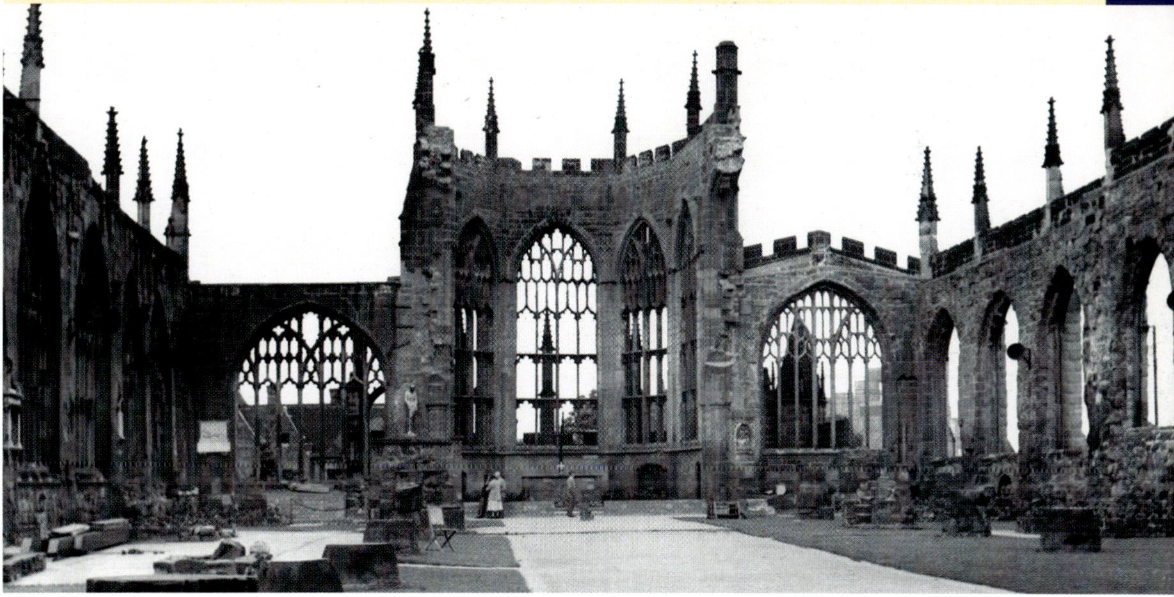

On the night of 14 November 1940, German bombs destroyed the ancient cathedral church of St Michael. It was only in 1962 that the Bishop of Coventry, in the presence of Queen Elizabeth II, finally consecrated the new cathedral built to replace it. During the intervening years the gaunt but still splendid ruins of the old building were left to stand, a lasting reminder of the folly of war.

11

COVENTRY, THE CATHEDRAL c1965 C169076

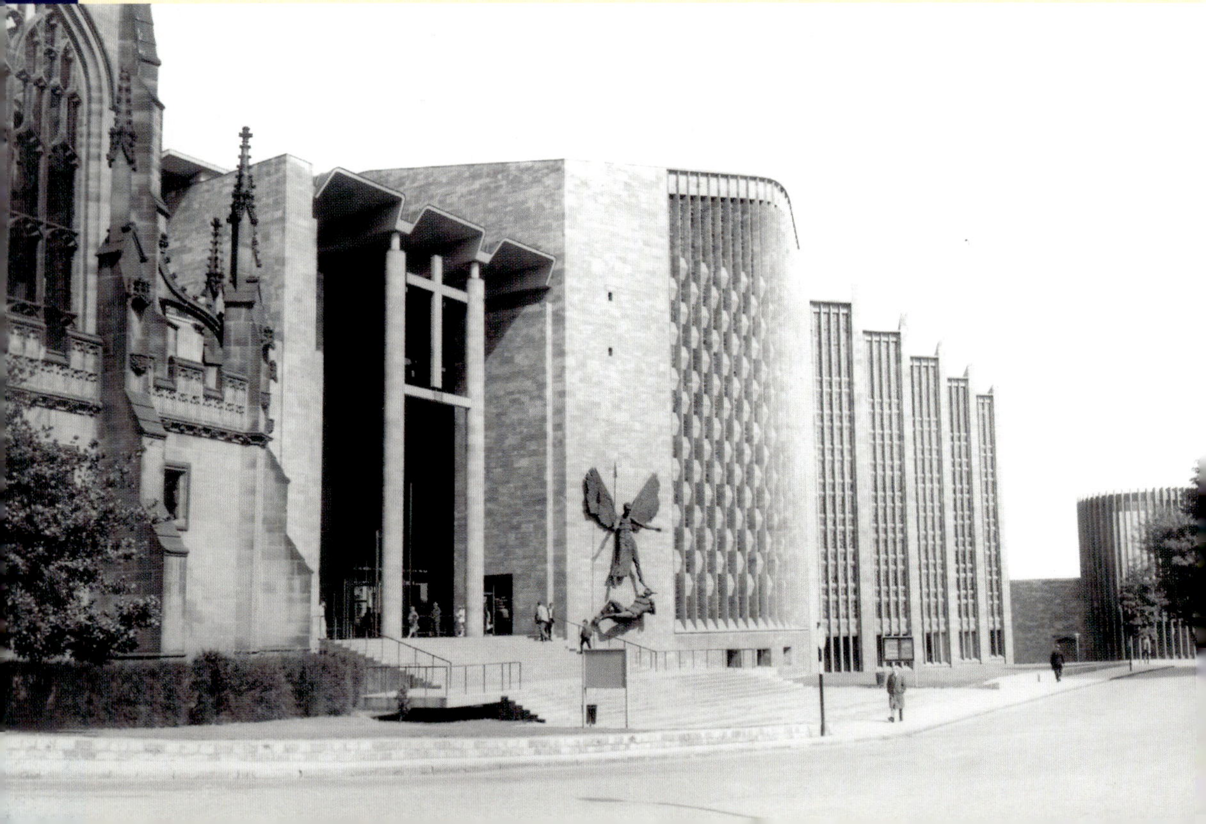

When Basil Spence designed Coventry's new cathedral, he incorporated the bombed ruins of the old St Michael's into the modern building; the old church became the new cathedral's vestibule. Spence said that his design came to him when he was under the influence of anaesthetic for toothache: he saw zigzagging walls and an altar ablaze with light. His use of curves and zigzags helped to disguise the fact that the nave of the new building was only 270 feet long and 80 feet wide, quite small in cathedral terms. The new cathedral is a symbol of Coventry's renewal after the blitz.

By the entrance is Epstein's sculpture of St Michael defeating Lucifer, one of his last works. The cathedral contains work by many contemporary artists, including Graham Sutherland and John Piper.

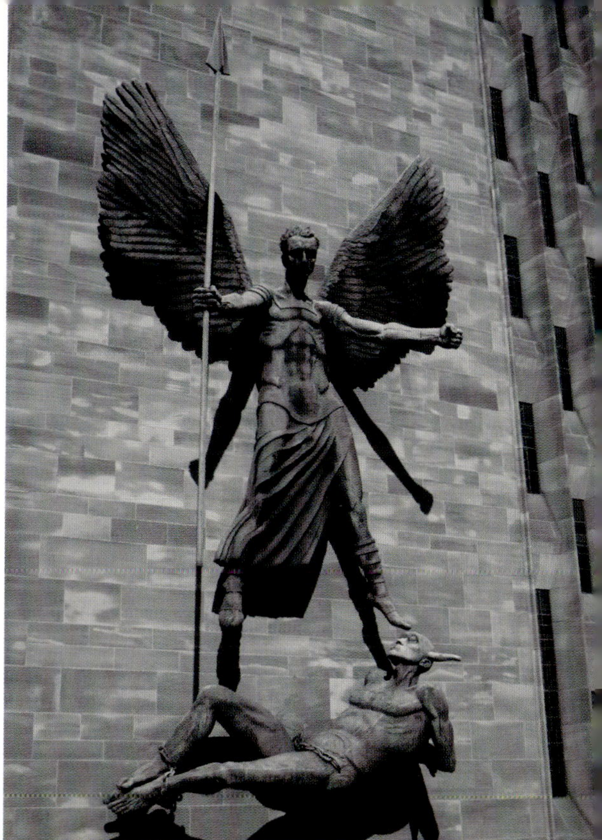

COVENTRY, THE STATUE ON THE CATHEDRAL 2004 C169743

13 DURHAM, THE CATHEDRAL FROM THE RIVER 1921 70712

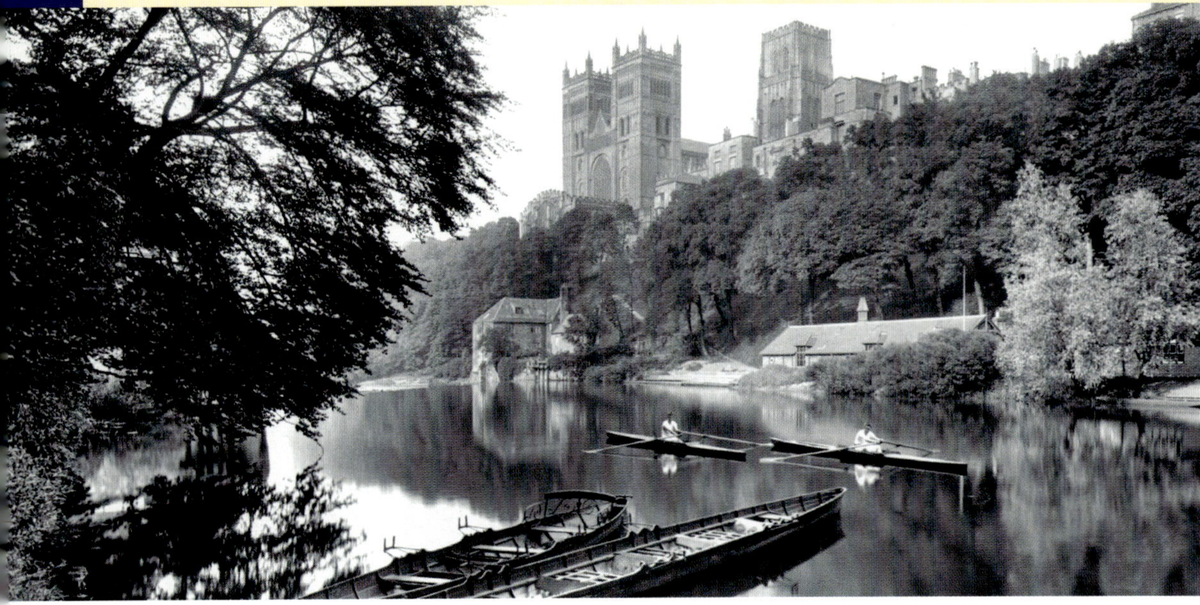

From all directions, the massive and magnificent Durham Cathedral dominates the landscape. It was built at various periods between the 11th and 13th centuries, and its great central tower was rebuilt between 1465 and 1495 after lightning and fire had destroyed its predecessor. The River Wear, once a vital part of the city's defences, is now used for more pleasurable purposes.

The impressive roof is the first example of rib vaulting in Europe. These richly carved choir stalls date from 1665; the original stalls and the font canopy had been burnt by Scots soldiers imprisoned in the cathedral after the battle of Dunbar in 1650. Above the high altar is the magnificent rose window, over 98 feet in circumference, depicting Christ surrounded by the twelve apostles and the twenty-four elders.

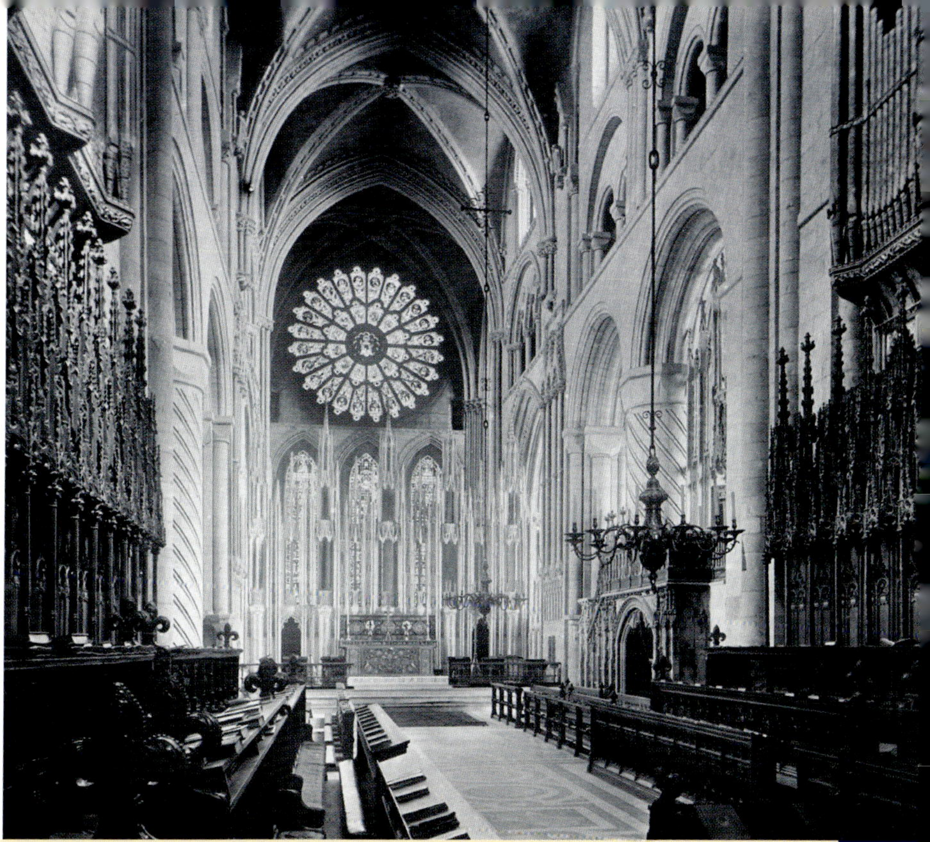

DURHAM, THE CATHEDRAL, THE CHOIR, LOOKING EAST 1892 30745

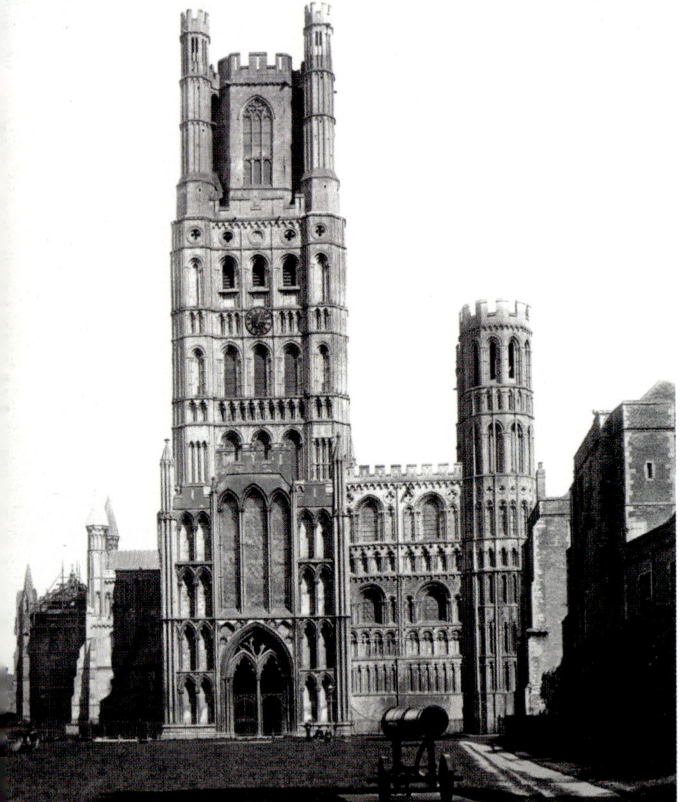

◄ *Ely Cathedral, which can be seen from up to twenty miles away on a clear day, is one of the most stirring sights in Fenland. Here we have the classic view of the west front, lop-sided in appearance since the north-west (left-hand) transept and tower fell in the late Middle Ages. The cannon in the foreground is a Russian one captured at Sebastopol in the 1850s.*

► *This photograph gives us a close view of the Octagon, 'a unique and arresting achievement of the Late Decorated period' (Alec Clifton-Taylor). This octagonal wooden lantern rises out of the larger stone octagonal tower, both of which were erected at the initiative of Alan of Walsingham, sacrist and later prior, after the original tower fell in 1322.*

ELY, THE CATHEDRAL c1878 10953

ELY, THE VIEW FROM THE WEST TOWER OF THE CATHEDRAL C1955 E34071

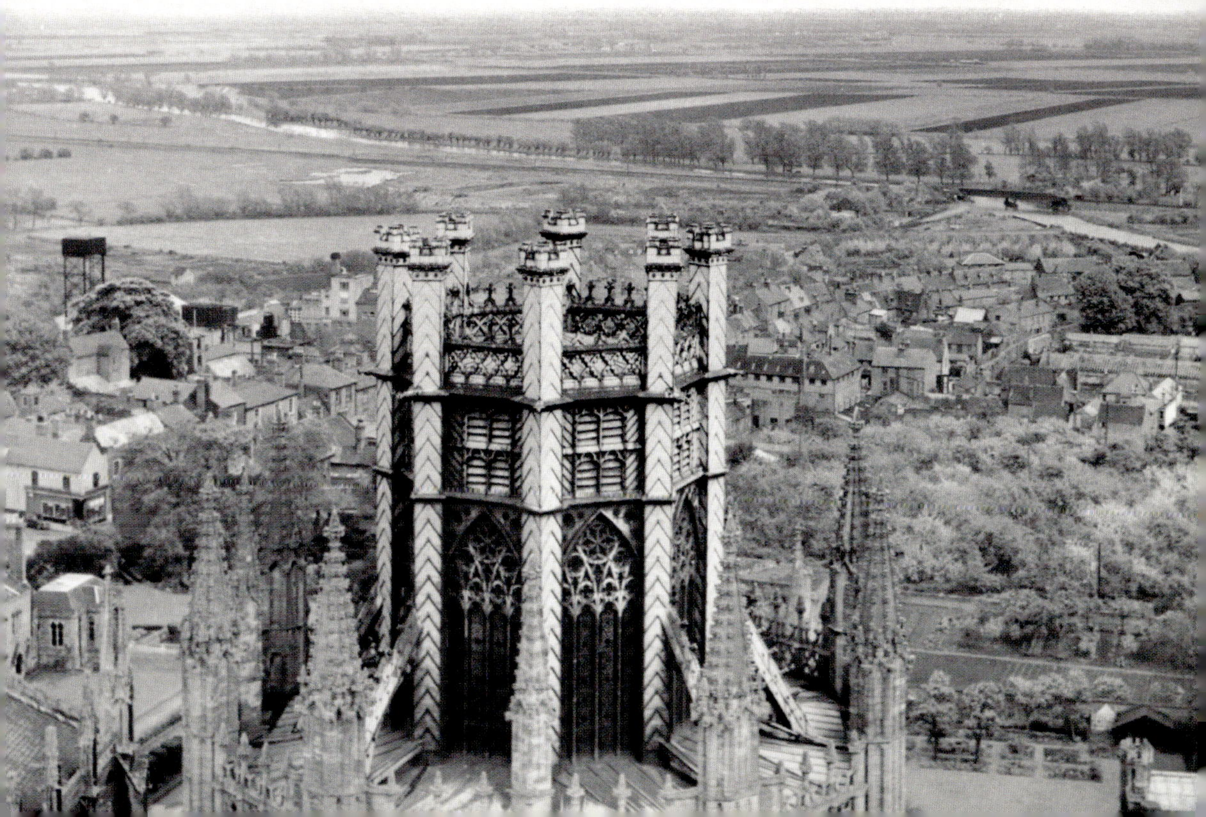

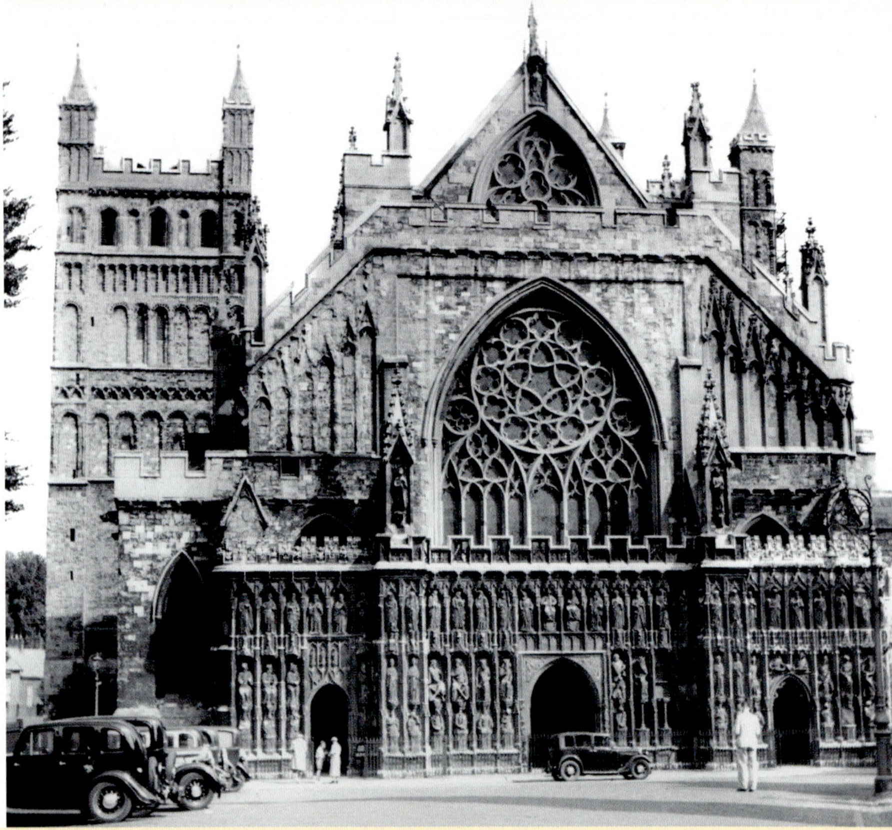

Exeter Cathedral's magnificent west front, carved with kings, priests and angels, dates from the 14th century. A statue of St Peter, the cathedral's patron saint, stands high on the gable. In this photograph, the cars, already period pieces to our eyes, serve to emphasise the timeless majesty of the building.

EXETER, THE CATHEDRAL, THE WEST FRONT c1950 E48011

EXETER, THE CATHEDRAL, THE NAVE, LOOKING EAST 1896 37998

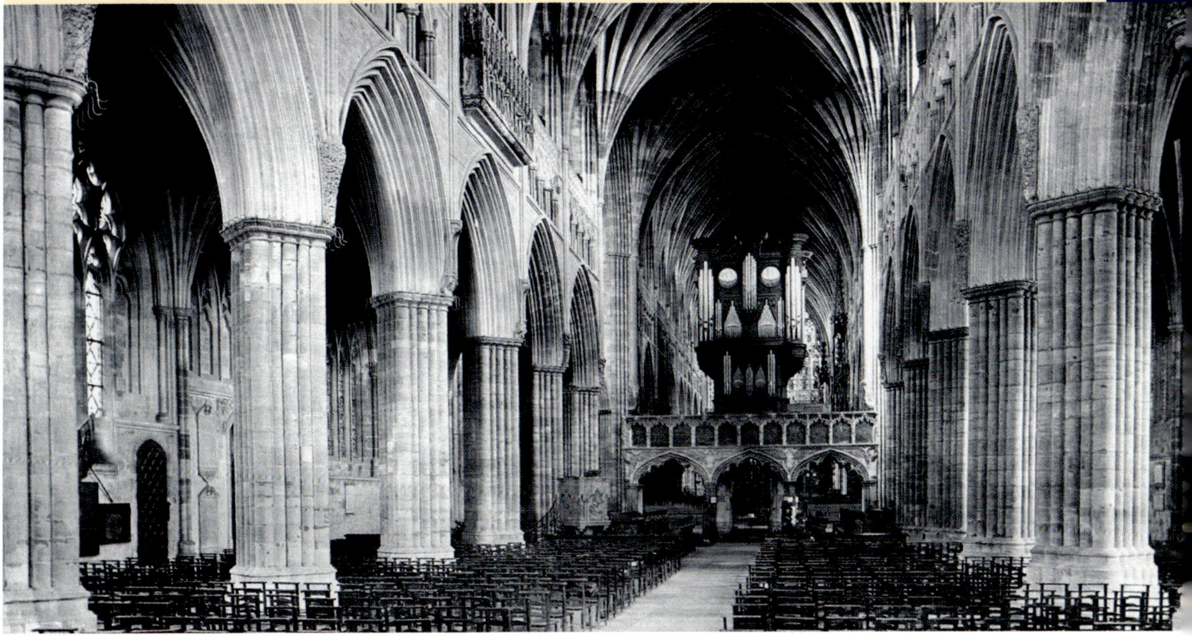

The interior of Exeter Cathedral is glorious. The tierceron ribbed vault 'is among the most magnificent creations of Gothic architecture in any country' (Alec Clifton-Taylor), and the richly moulded and carved pillars and arches lead the eye towards the original pulpitum, or stone screen, which dates from the early 14th century.

This photograph shows sheep grazing in what is now almost the city centre. Gloucester Cathedral has a Norman nave, later Gothic vaulting, an early Perpendicular choir and a later Perpendicular Lady Chapel; yet these disparate architectural styles form a coherent whole.

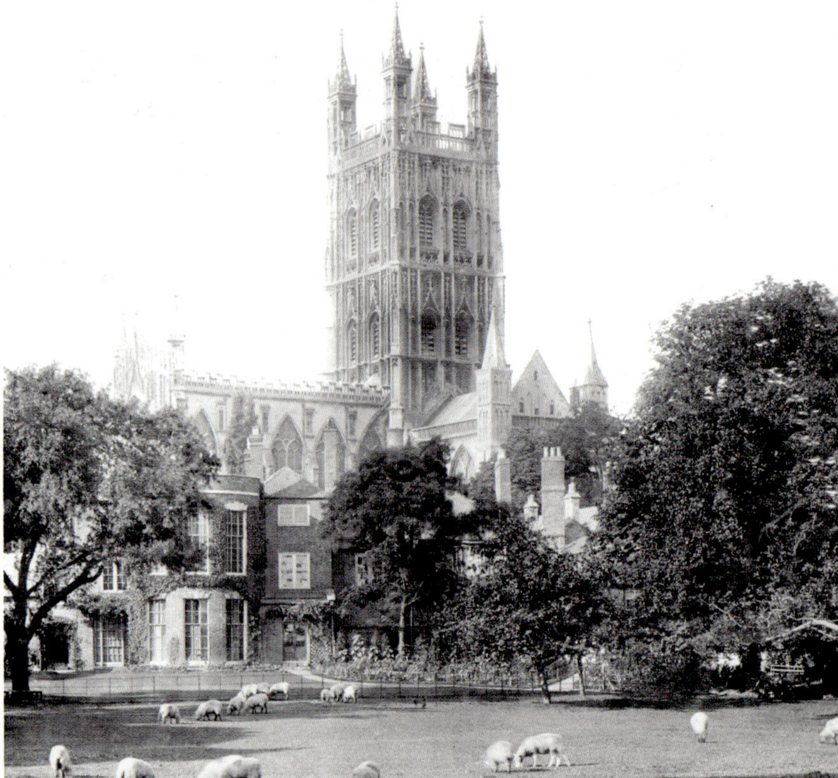

GLOUCESTER, THE CATHEDRAL FROM THE NORTH EAST 1891 28970

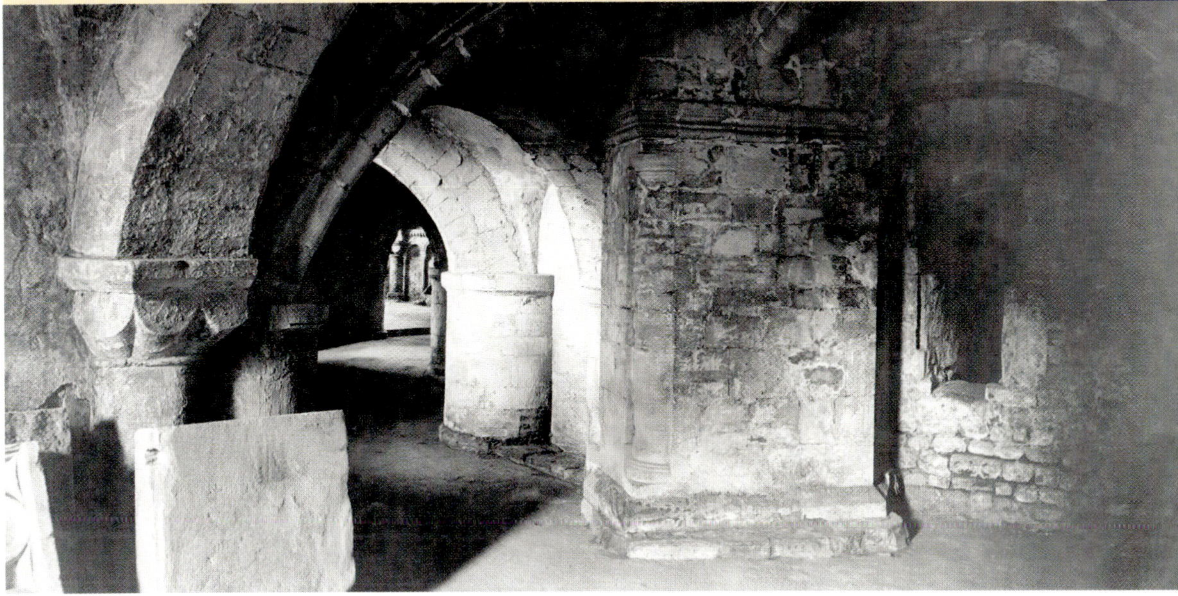

The crypt contains clear differences in its building style. The original design proved too weak to carry the weight imposed upon it. Ealdred, Bishop of Worcester, was involved in the initial construction in the mid 11th century, and it is probable that Serlo, Abbot of Gloucester from 1072, did the strengthening work. The Norman masons' marks are clear to see.

HEREFORD, THE CATHEDRAL FROM THE SOUTH WEST 1891 29270

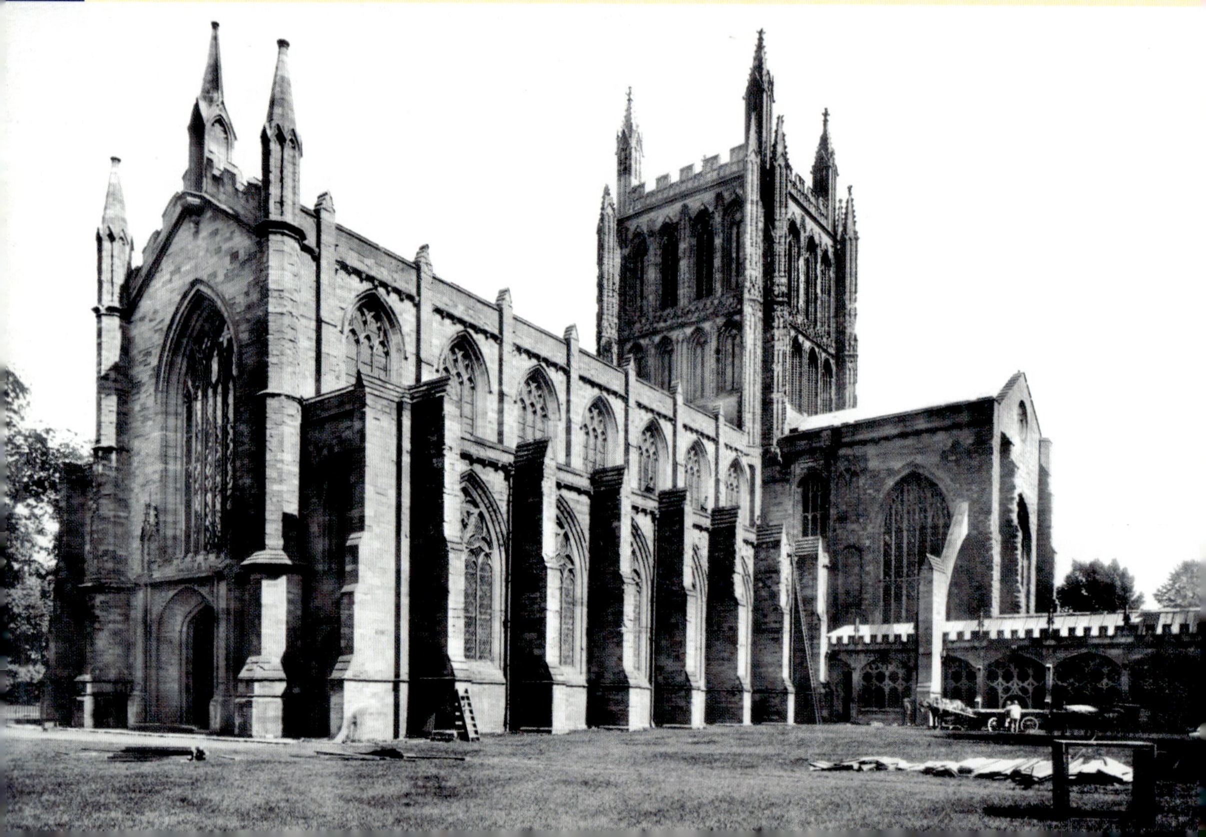

This interesting photograph shows Hereford Cathedral before the reconstruction and considerable embellishment of the west front by Wyatt, which was completed in 1908. The original west front collapsed along with its tower on Easter Monday 1786, bringing down much of the nave with it. The massive noble central tower dates from c1325.

This chained library is the finest in the world, containing books and manuscripts that date back a thousand years and more. Chaining the books was an important security measure. It enabled people to read the books on the ledge below, while ensuring that they could not be taken away - in medieval times, books were rare and costly items. A new chained library and accompanying exhibition was opened by Queen Elizabeth II in 1996.

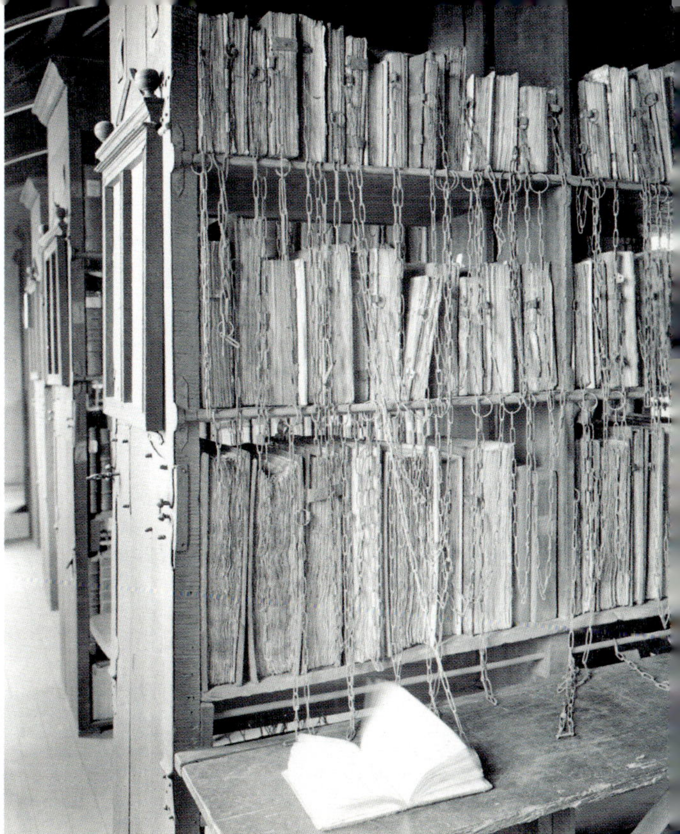

HEREFORD, THE CATHEDRAL, THE CHAINED LIBRARY 1925 77352

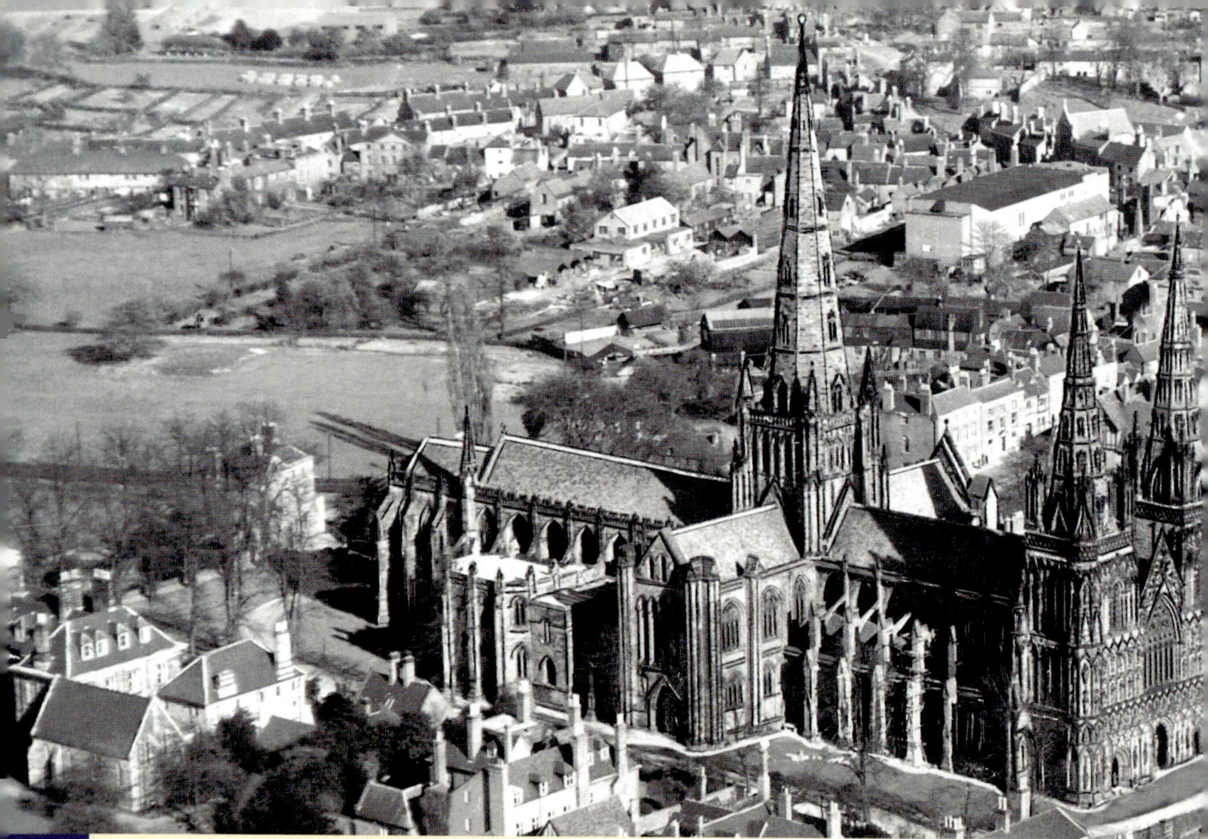

23

LICHFIELD, THE CATHEDRAL c1955 L45052

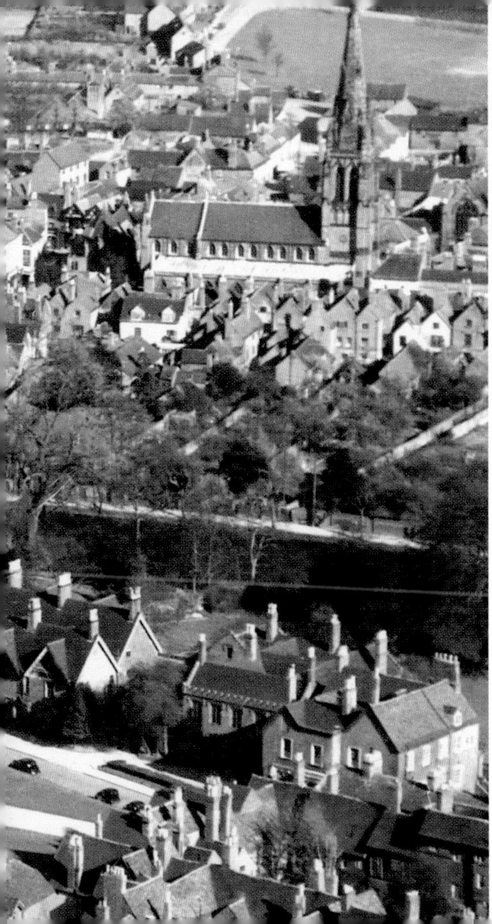

Work on Lichfield Cathedral began in the late 12th century, and took about 150 years to complete, though additional work was undertaken during the 15th century. The three stone spires are known as the Ladies of the Vale. The cathedral was badly damaged during the Civil War: the central spire was all but destroyed, and much of the building was left roofless.

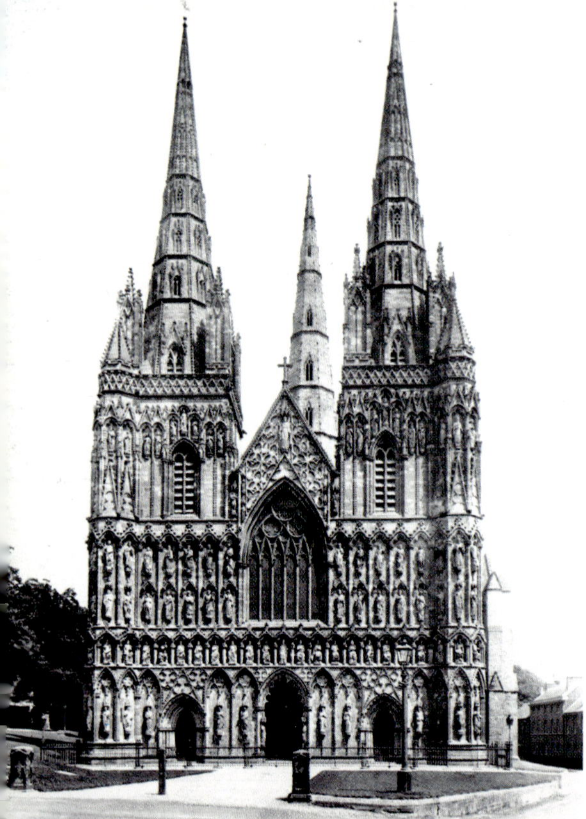

The west front of Lichfield Cathedral dates from the Decorated period, but most of this amazing display of sculpture is Victorian – only five statues high up on the north-west tower are original. The central doors have beautiful scrolled wrought iron hinges dating from c1300. During the Civil War, the cathedral and the close were held for the King; the rest of the city declared for Parliament.

This marvellously atmospheric view along the High Street looks across towards Lincoln's great medieval minster church which dominates the city and the countryside for miles around – the beautiful central tower is the tallest of the Middle Ages in England after the Boston Stump. The cathedral retains some Norman work, but most of it dates from the 13th century, with additions of the 14th century.

LICHFIELD, THE CATHEDRAL, THE WEST FRONT 1887 20222

LINCOLN, THE CATHEDRAL AND STONEBOW 1890 25654

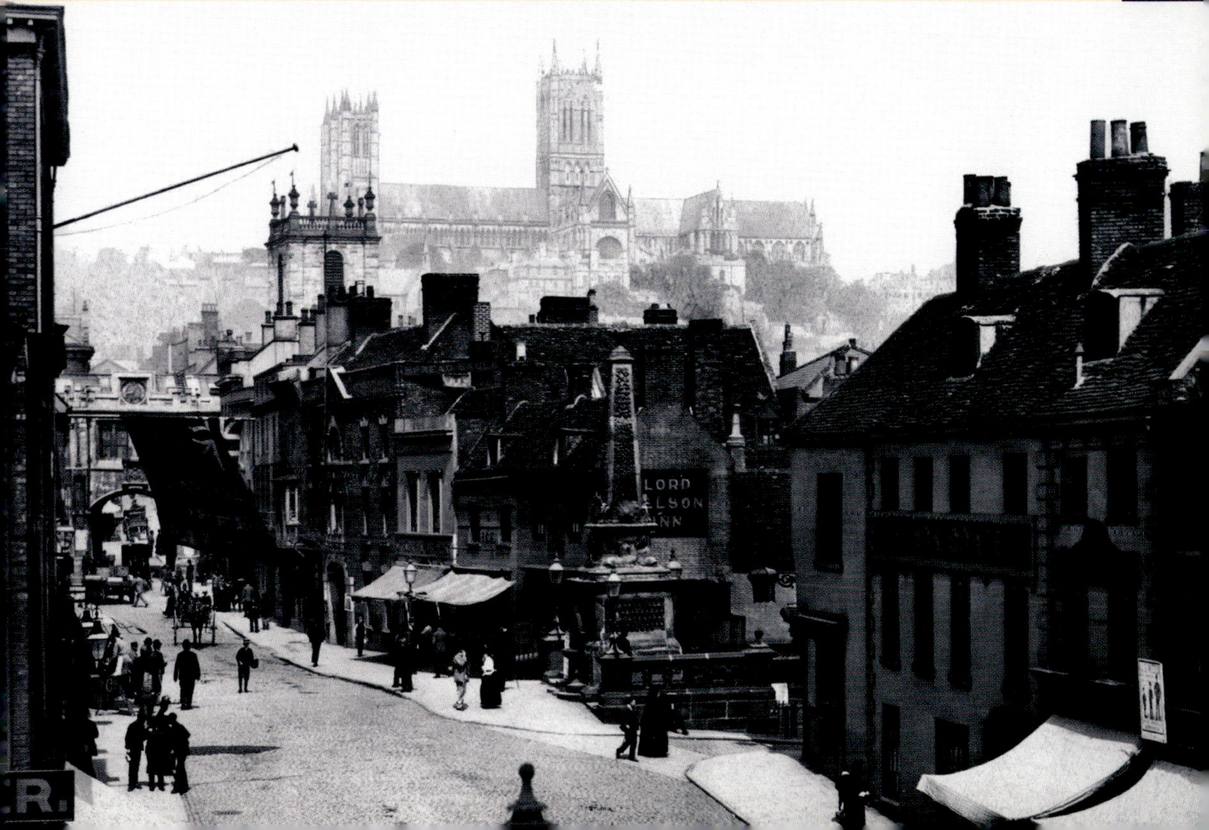

26 LINCOLN, THE CATHEDRAL, THE SOUTH PORCH 1895 35547

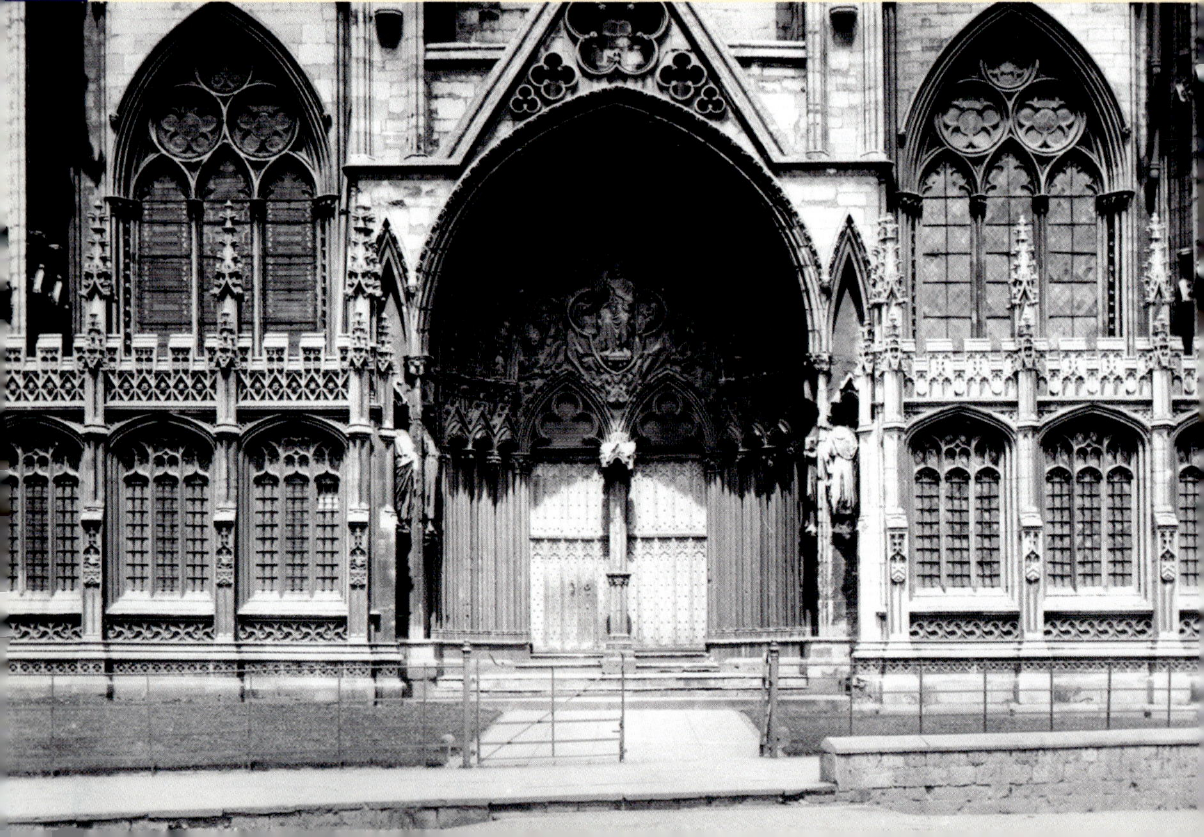

◀ *Known as the Judgement Porch from its carved scenes of the Last Judgement, the south porch of Lincoln Cathedral led into the richly carved Angel Choir, the east arm of the cathedral built for St Hugh's shrine; it was probably used by pilgrims, who would leave by the north porch opposite. It was built about 1260, but it has been much renewed. A statue of the Virgin and Child from the 1930s now occupies the central niche.*

▶ *Perched on the summit of Ludgate Hill at almost the highest point in the city, Wren's masterpiece of St Paul's Cathedral is the pride of London. A train has just left Holborn Viaduct Station and thunders south over the bridge, steam ballooning out over the roofs. Below, traffic crawls miserably up Ludgate Hill. In wet weather the road became a quagmire and horses pulling heavy wagons slipped and slid up to St Paul's.*

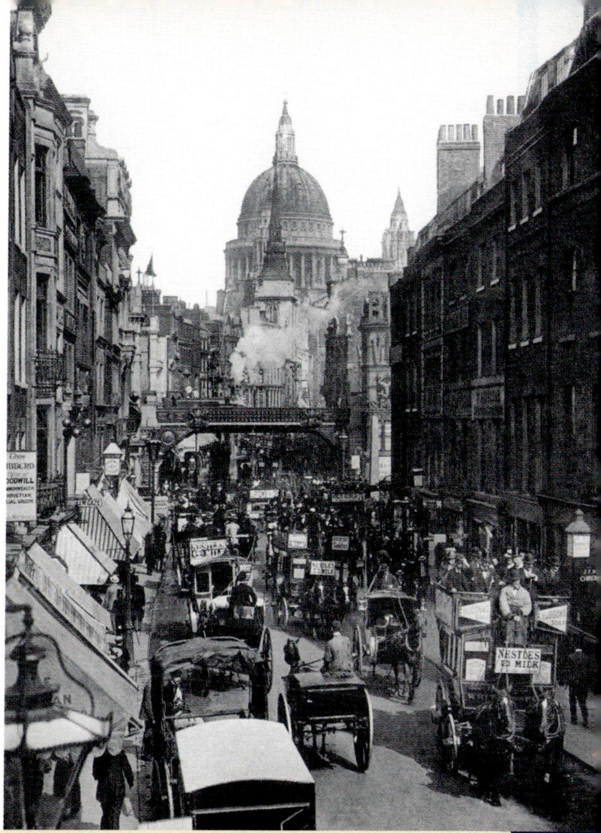

LONDON, ST PAUL'S CATHEDRAL AND LUDGATE HILL 1897 L130037

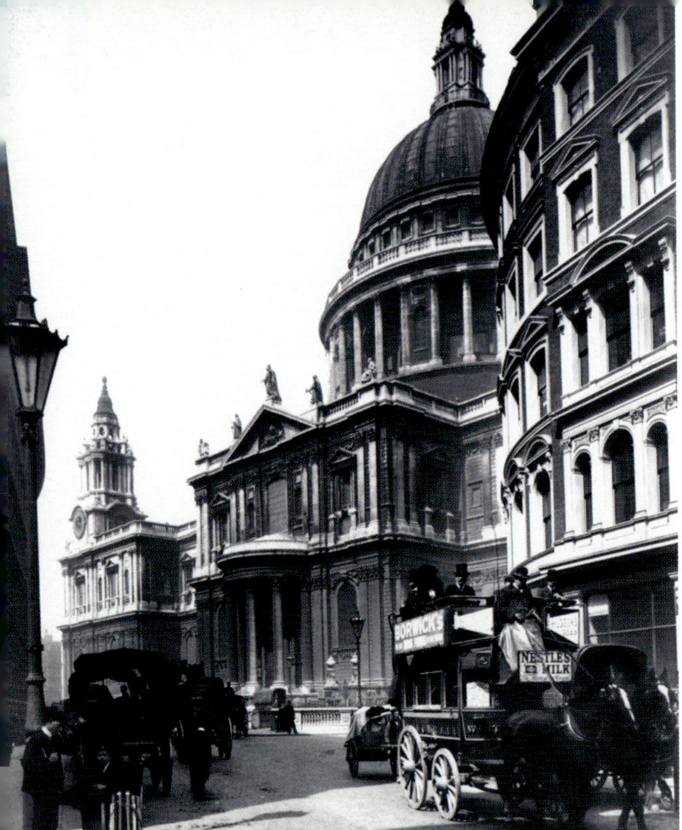

◄ *The magnificent elevations of St Paul's, built in the Corinthian style, soar above the surrounding streets and the horse-drawn vehicles. Wren directed its construction at such a ponderous pace that Parliament cut his salary from £200 to £100 a year. It was not until 1711, when the work was finally completed, that he was paid the balance owing.*

► *The great late 15th-century spire of Norwich Cathedral soars to 315 feet, the second highest spire in England. Its predecessor was blown through the choir roof in a great gale in 1362. The medieval Watergate was restored and roofed in 1947. The lane to Lower Close was originally a canal, used for carrying stone for building the cathedral in the 12th century.*

LONDON, ST PAUL'S CATHEDRAL FROM CANNON STREET 1905 L130164

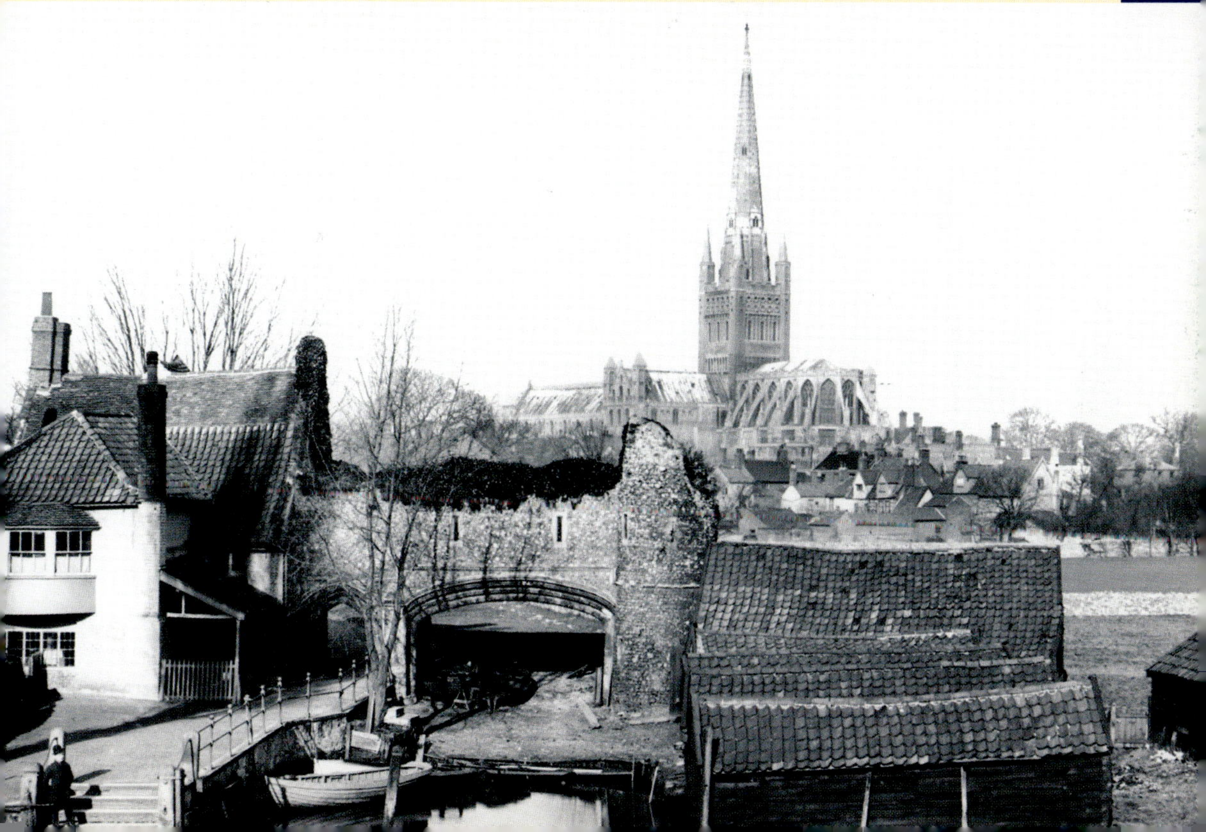

Norwich's choir stalls date from 1420; but up to 1515 they had more than their fair share of fires, necessitating rearrangements, renewals, repairs and additions. The great Norman crossing tower has windows high up, which flood the crossing with light. Beyond the crossing, the network of 15th-century vault ribs recedes into the distance.

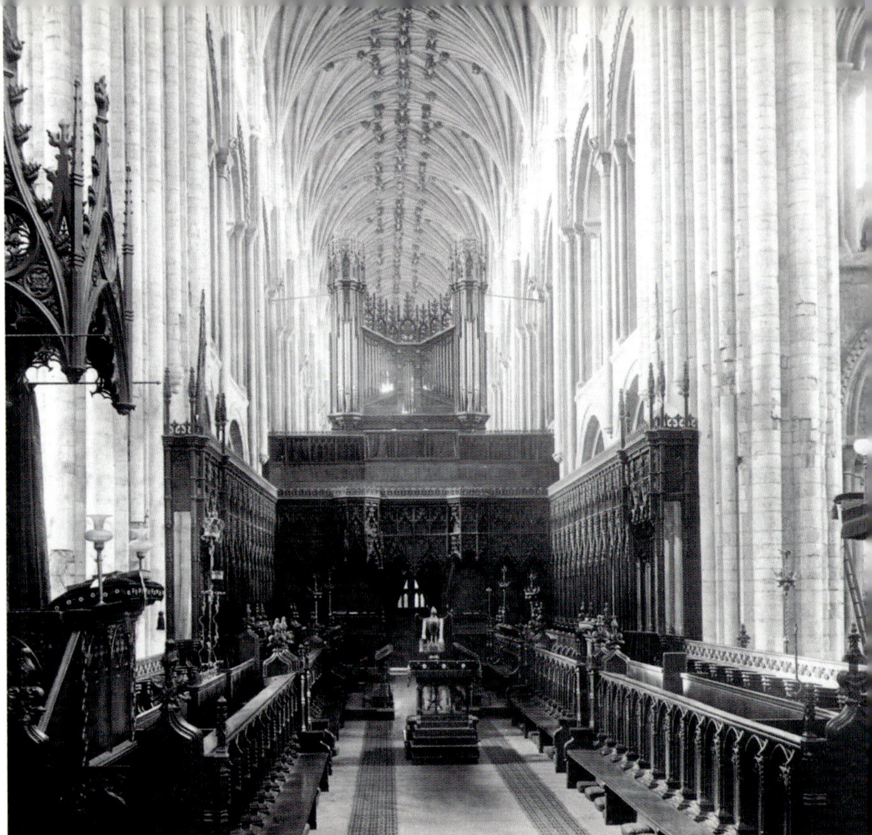

NORWICH, THE CATHEDRAL, THE CHOIR WEST 1891 28152

PETERBOROUGH, MARKET SQUARE 1919 69081

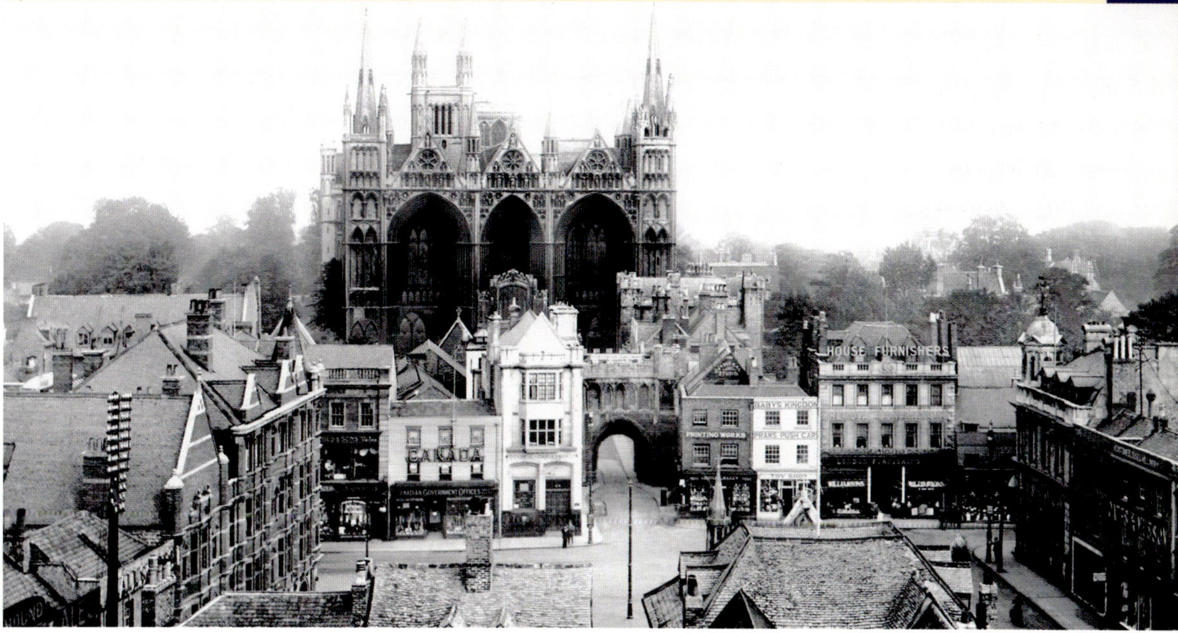

This atmospheric photograph, taken from St John's Church, shows Peterborough Cathedral's bulk rising above the rooftops. We have a good view of the striking and dramatic west front with its trio of huge arches, richly moulded and recessed into the façade, dating from c1220. The central Galilee porch and the little spires were added in the late 14th century.

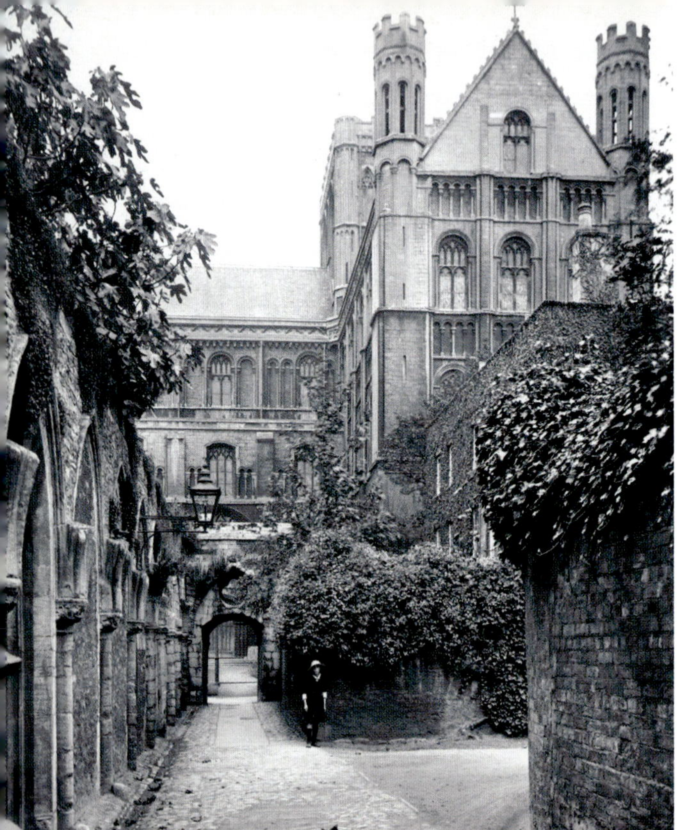

◄ *The slip, or slype, is a narrow passage between the cloisters and Laurel Court, the school where Nurse Edith Cavell taught. She was a heroine of the First World War, condemned to death and shot by firing squad in 1915 for helping prisoners escape. Above the slip, the cathedral soars, its architectural details showing its Norman origins.*

► *Ripon Cathedral stands on the site of the Saxon abbey church of St Wilfrid, of which this crypt still remains. It dates from about 672, and is one of the oldest Christian survivals in England. The passages are very narrow – indeed, one passage, thought to have been a confessional, is called 'the needle'. The crypt may also have been used to store religious relics which St Wilfrid brought back from Rome.*

PETERBOROUGH, THE CATHEDRAL, THE SLIP 1919 69085

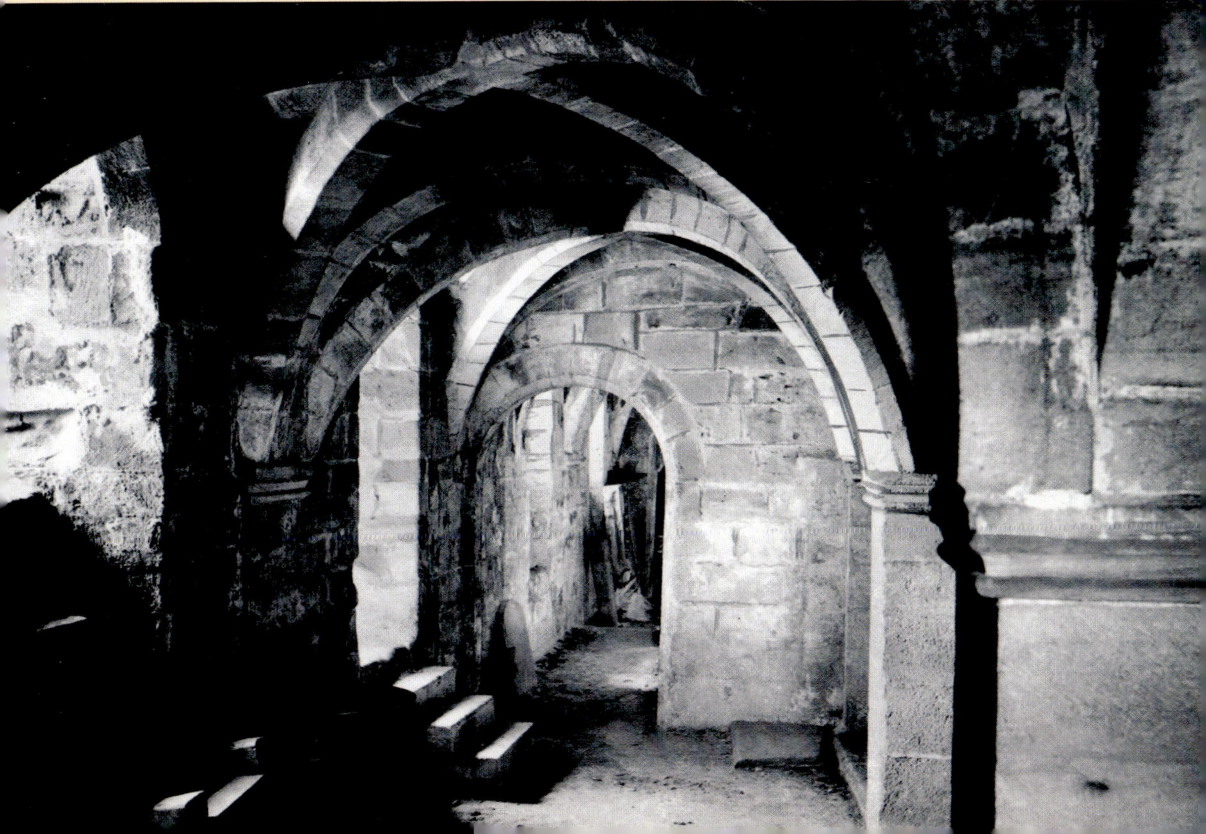

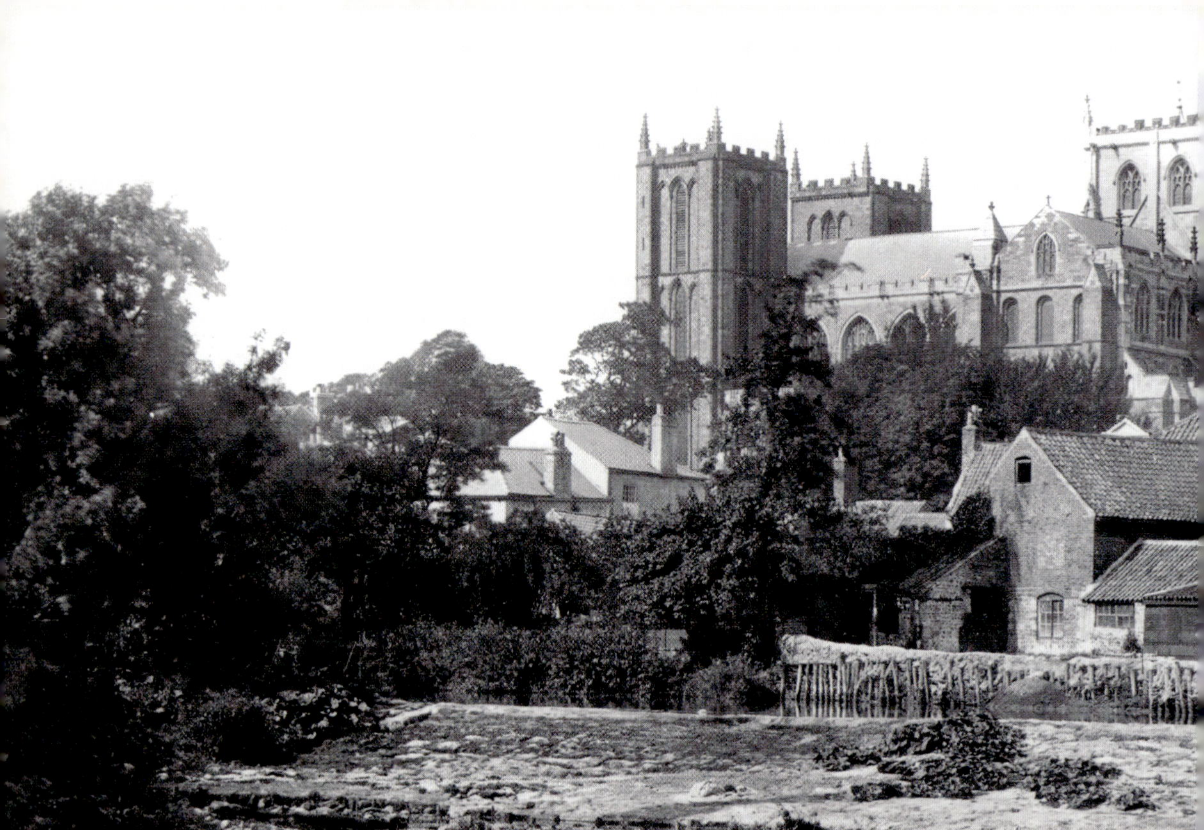

RIPON, THE CATHEDRAL C1885 18316

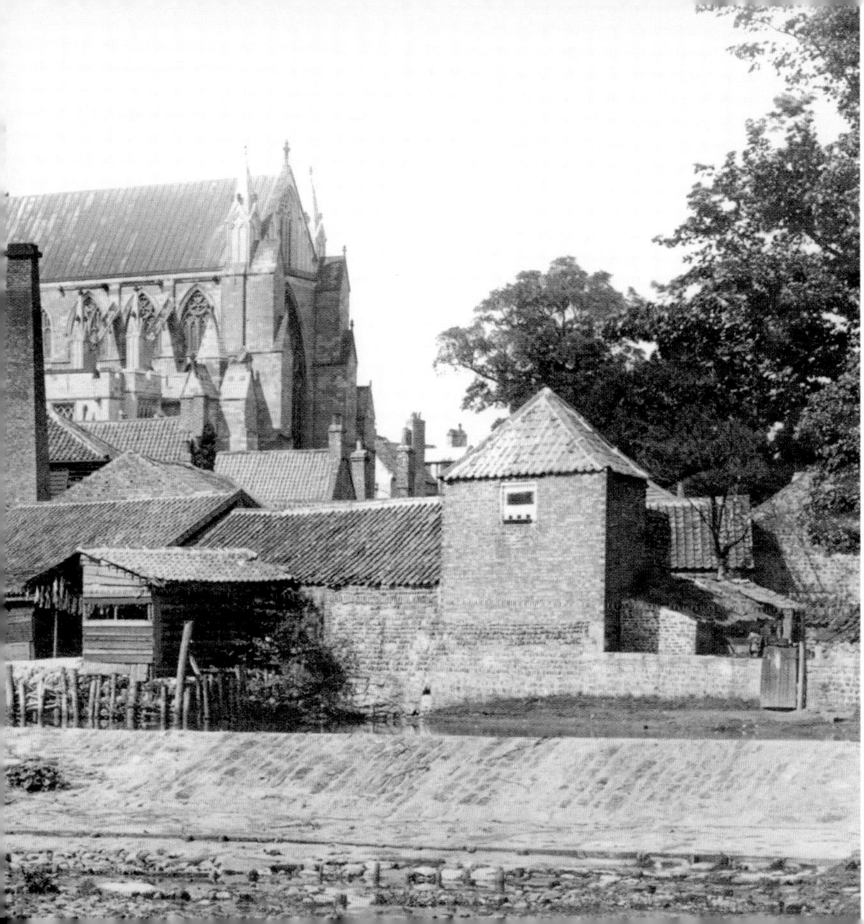

Ripon Cathedral was begun in the 12th century, and was enlarged, altered and repaired over the centuries. The wood carving in the choir, dating from the 14th century, depicts many fantastic creatures. When Lewis Carroll was visiting his father, who was Canon of Ripon from 1852 to 1868, these wonderful carvings inspired his book 'Alice's Adventures in Wonderland'.

ROCHESTER, THE CATHEDRAL 1894 34012

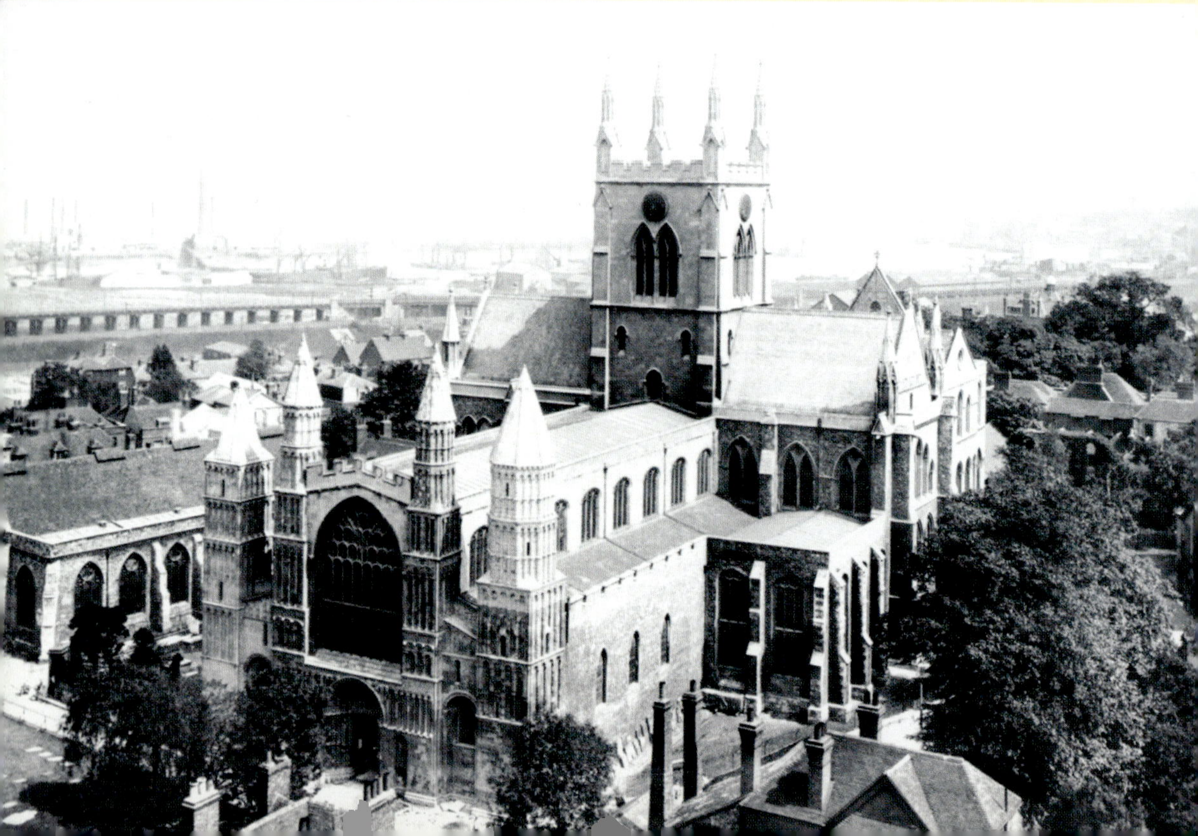

◄ *Rochester Cathedral, founded in 604, is second only to Canterbury in age. It was rebuilt by the Normans, who also built Rochester's castle, from which we view the cathedral in this photograph. The central tower was rebuilt in 1904 and crowned with a spire.*

► *At the foot of Boley Hill stands the 15th-century College Gate, one of three surviving entrances to the precincts of the cathedral, whose modest spire (added when the tower was rebuilt in 1904) rises behind. Next door, the Gate House Tea Rooms boasts some lovely 16th-century linenfold panelling.*

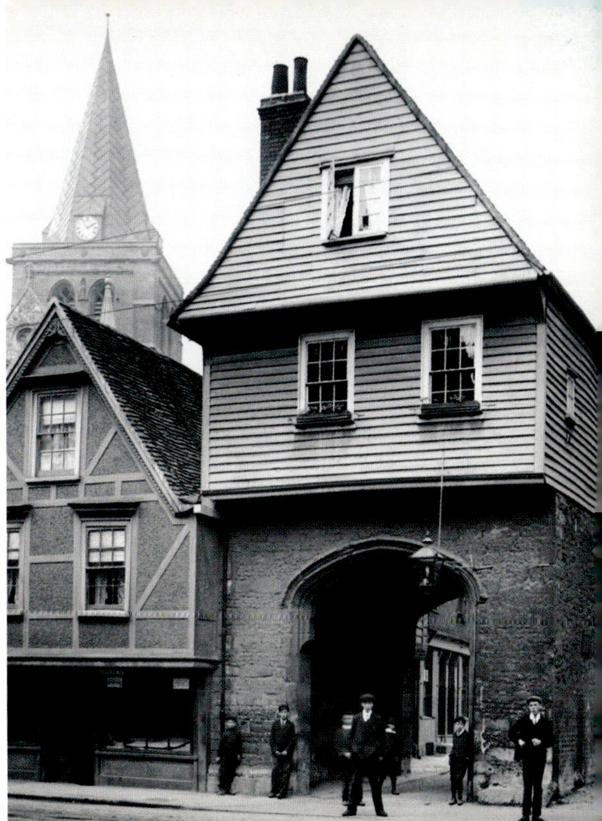

ROCHESTER, COLLEGE GATE AND THE CATHEDRAL 1908 59881

ST ALBANS, THE CATHEDRAL 1921 70455

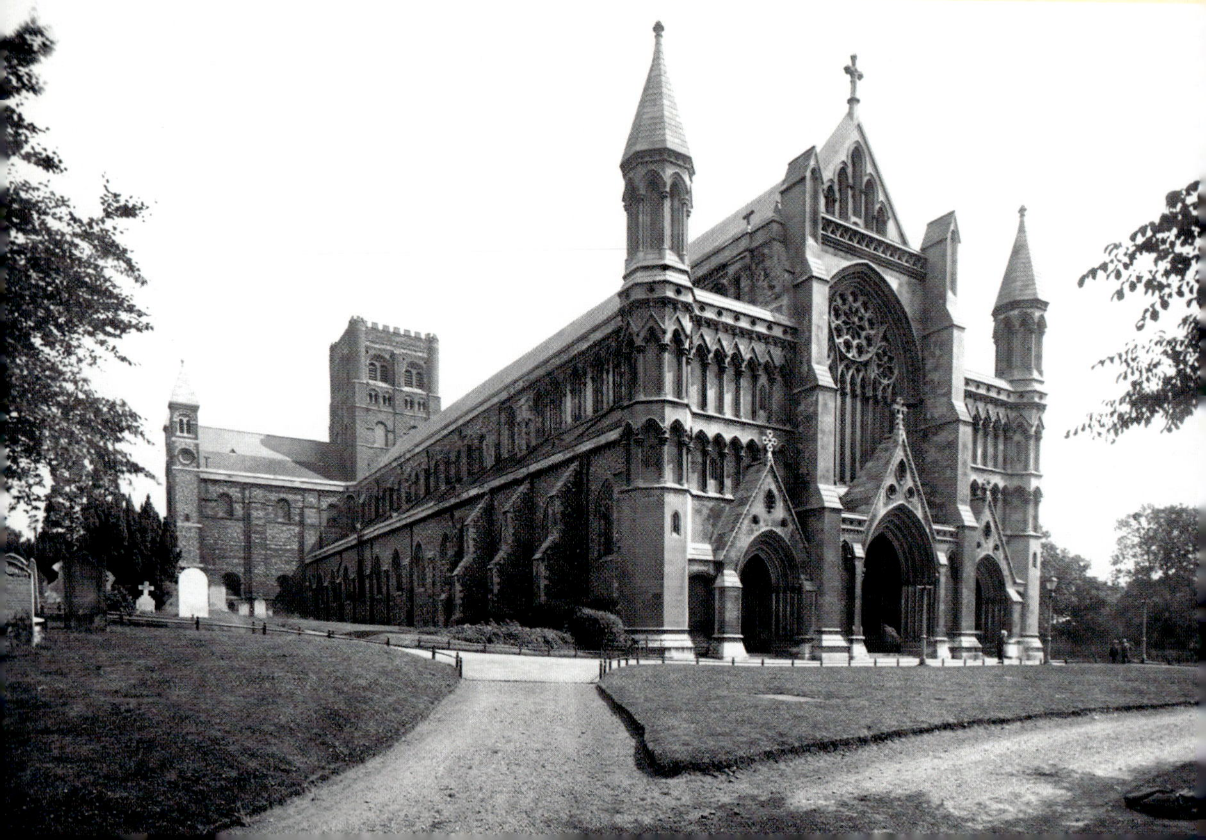

◄ *This view from the north west clearly illustrates the enormous length of St Albans Cathedral, which is longer than any in England except for Winchester. This Norman abbey church fell into disrepair in the 18th and 19th centuries, and considerable restoration work has been done here – it had been completed only about forty years before this photograph was taken.*

► *In the days when this was an abbey church, the ornate door on the right, the abbot's door, was part of the monks' processional route from the choir to the cloisters, which were located in the corner of the nave and the south transept, the most sheltered part of the monastic buildings.*

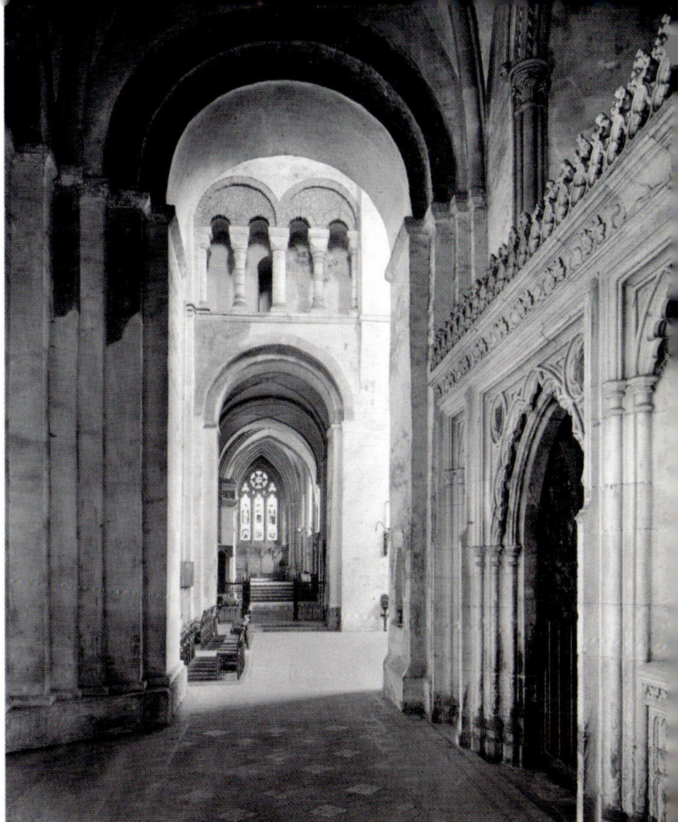

ST ALBANS, THE CATHEDRAL, SOUTH CHOIR AISLE 1921 70467

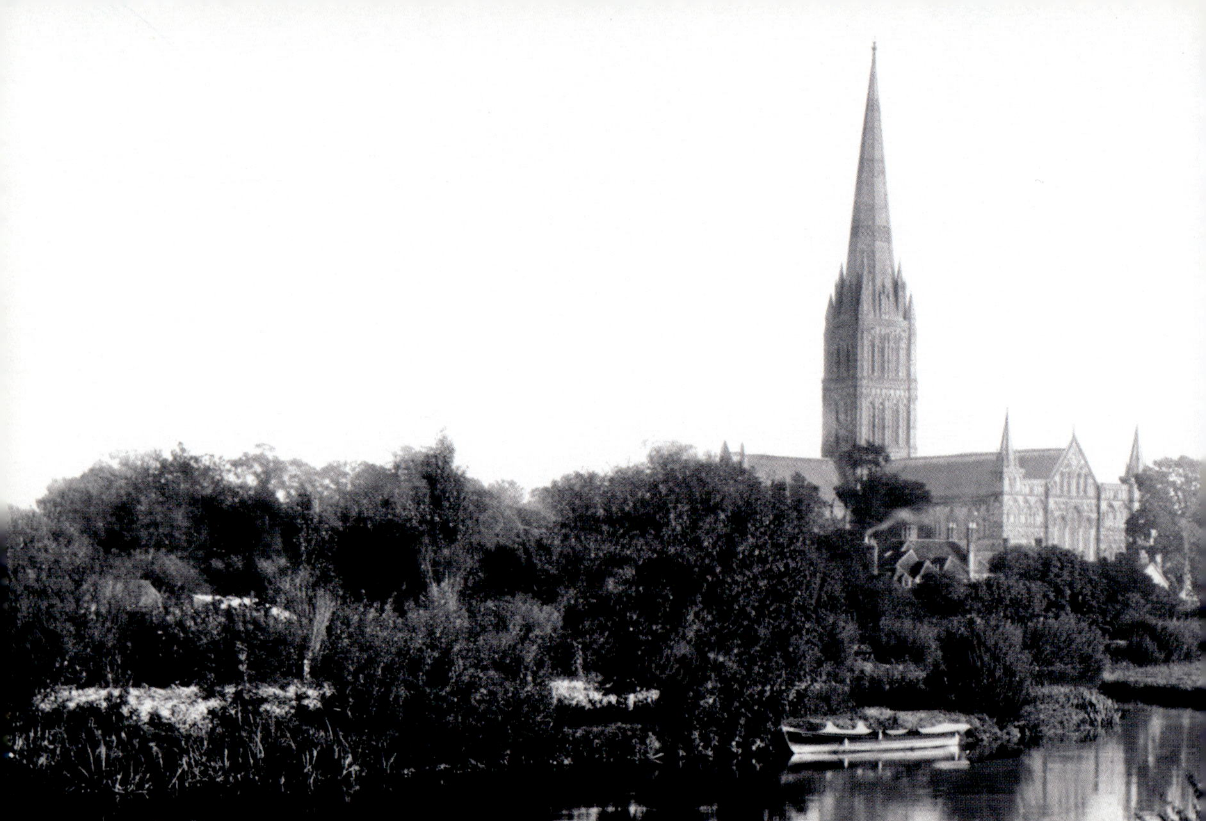

39

SALISBURY, THE CATHEDRAL FROM THE RIVER 1887 19730

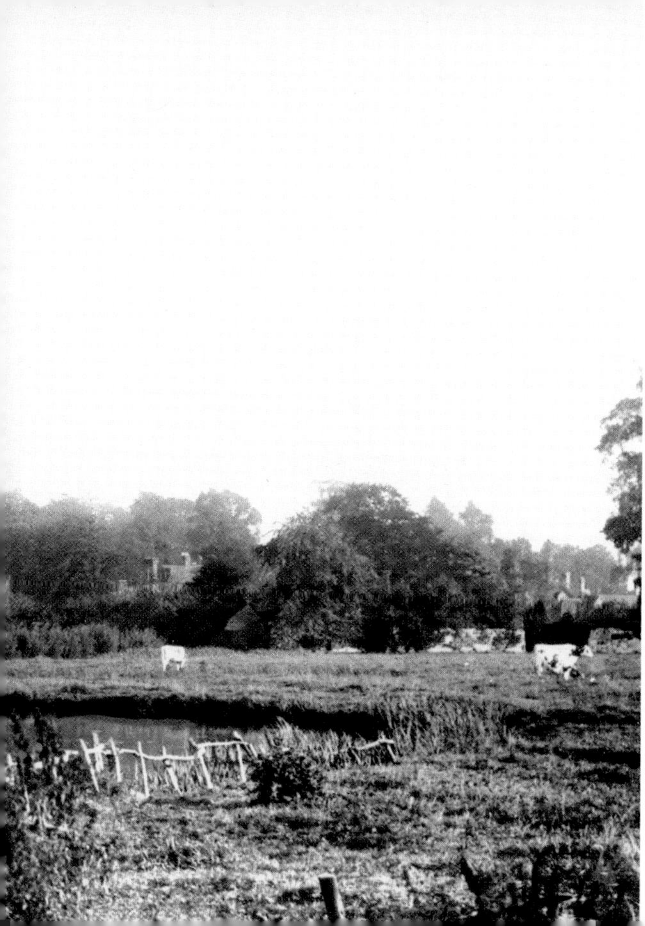

This classic view of Salisbury Cathedral has changed little in over a hundred years. The tranquil surface of the River Avon gently reflects the majesty of the cathedral and its incomparably magnificent 404-foot spire, the tallest in England. The famous water meadows on the right still exist; the fields on the left are now the Queen Elizabeth Gardens.

The main body of Salisbury Cathedral was completed in a short span of forty years between 1220 and 1260, so the interior has an impressive architectural unity. The light Chilmark limestone, quarried only ten miles away, contrasts with the dark Purbeck marble of the slender shafts supporting the arches. To the right we can see the canopy of the Bishop's seat.

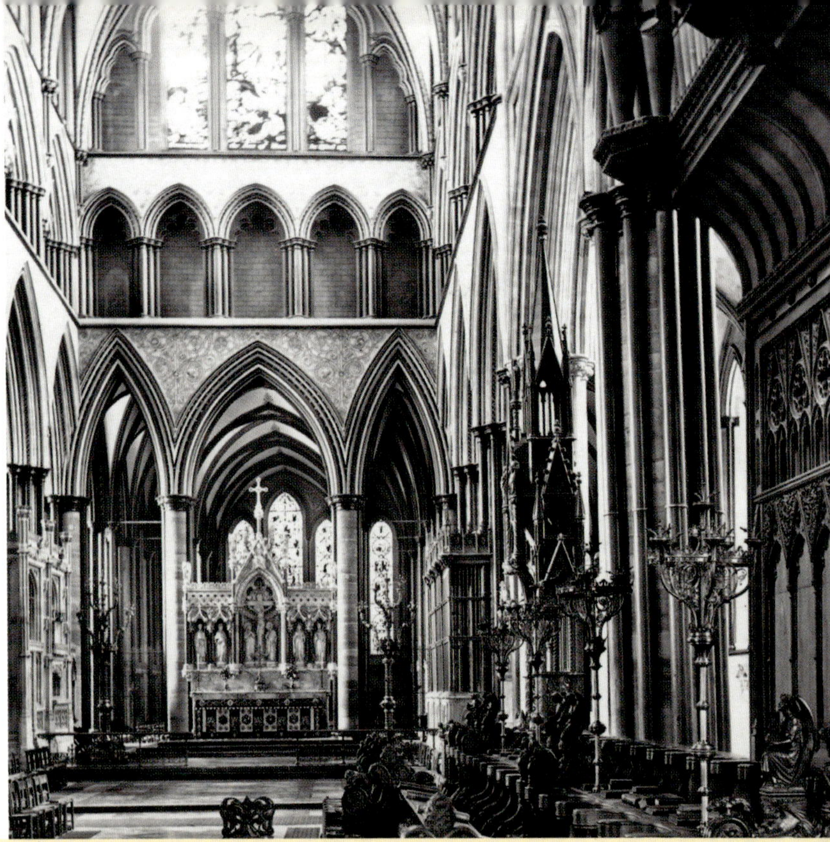

SALISBURY, THE CATHEDRAL, THE CHOIR EAST 1887 19764

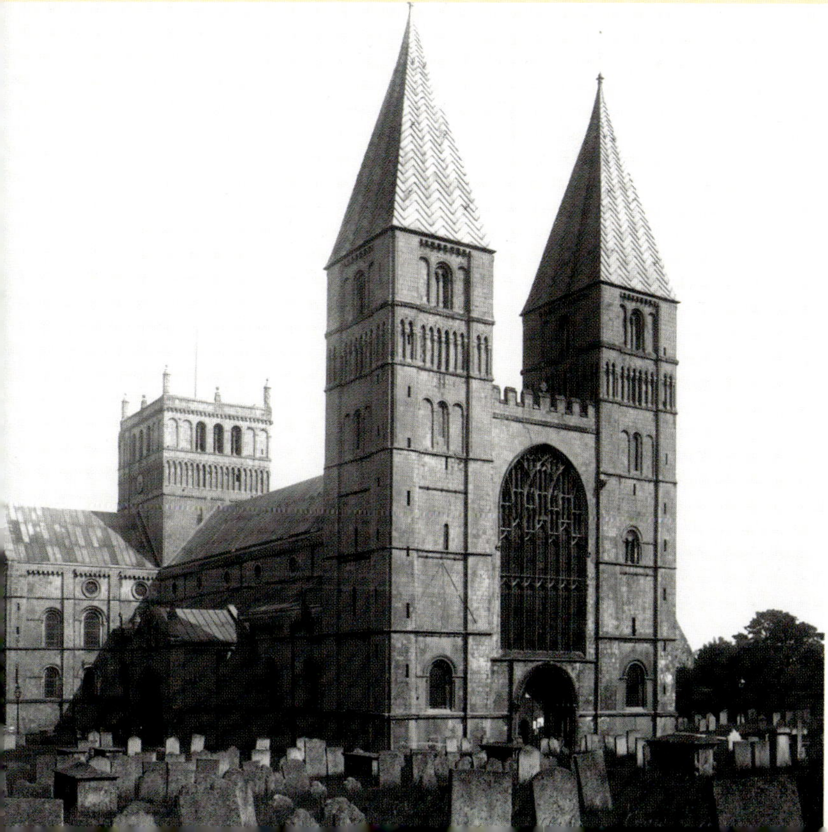

This superb minster church was founded before 956; the present church was started in 1108 by the Archbishop of York, and the west towers were completed by about 1150. Pairs of Norman west towers rarely survive intact; this example is even rarer in having Norman leaded pyramidal roofs. Admittedly, these are replicas dating from 1880 – the originals burned down in 1711. Southwell Minster became the Cathedral Church of the diocese in 1884.

SOUTHWELL, THE MINSTER AND THE BISHOP'S PALACE 1920 69456

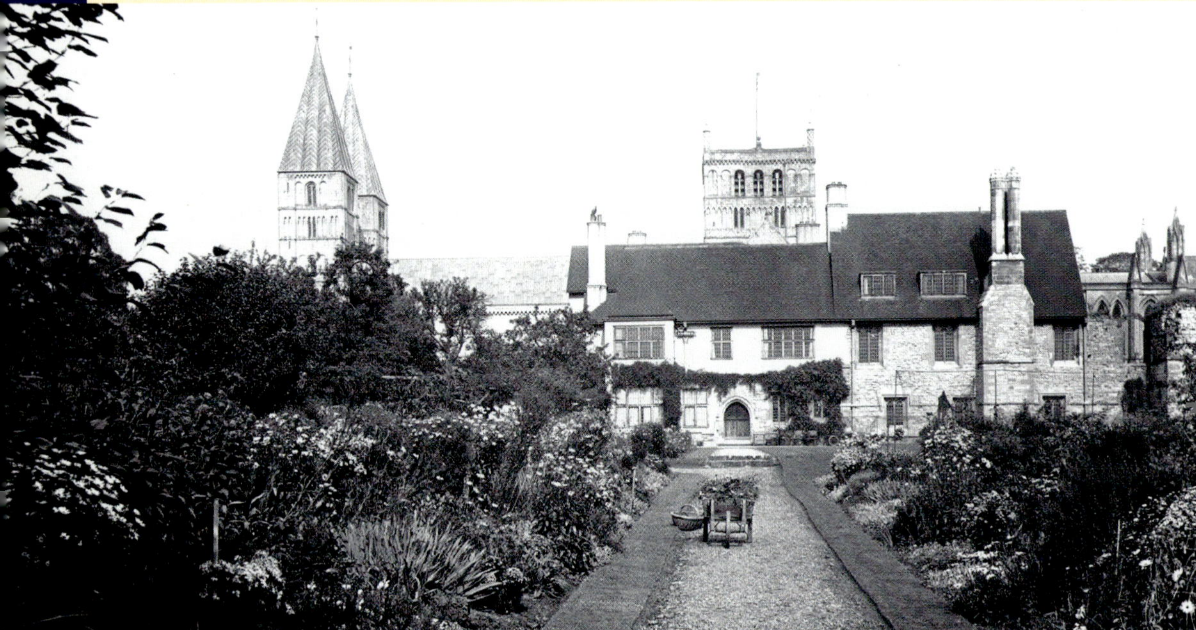

How fitting it is to view the cathedral from the bishop's garden: the Gothic foliage carvings in the chapter house are justly famous. The Bishop's Palace occupies the west half of the Archbishop of York's palace, which was rebuilt in the 14th century. The rest of the building is now open to the sky and used as a walled garden.

Wells Cathedral was begun in the 1180s and finished in the 1230s; its glory is its magnificent west front, surely the finest in the country, which has over 400 carved figures in its niches. Above are the grand 14th-century west towers, and beyond soars the great central tower, 'outstanding even in Somerset, a county famed for the splendour of its church towers' (Alec Clifton-Taylor).

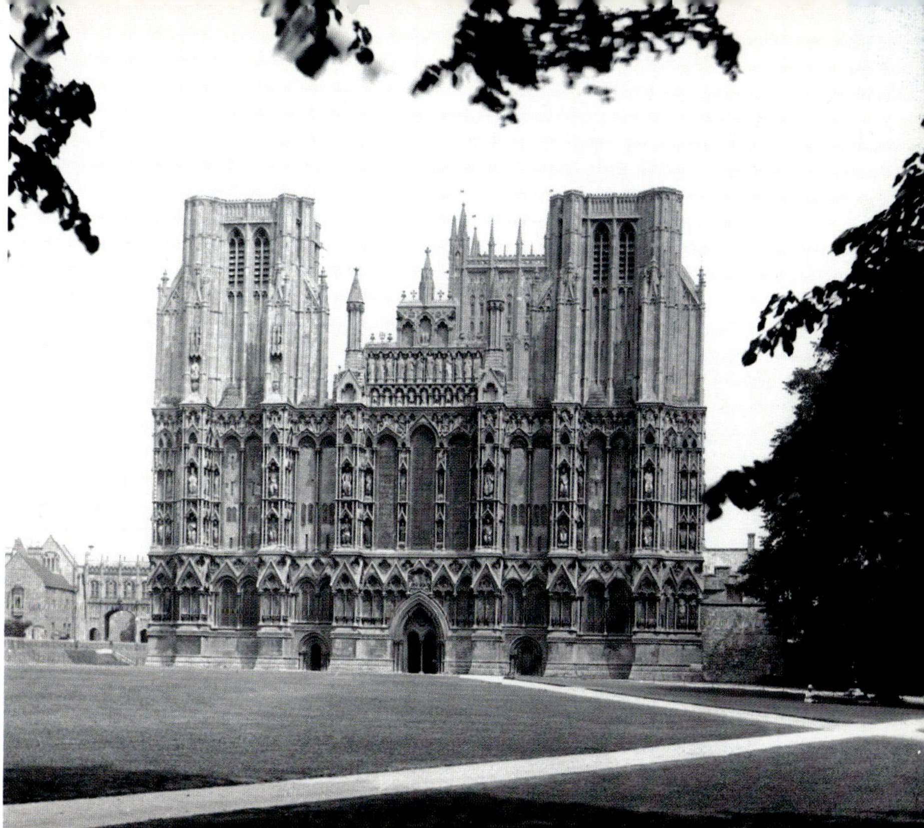

WELLS, THE CATHEDRAL, THE WEST FRONT 1923 73993

WELLS, THE BISHOP'S PALACE RUINS 1890 23895

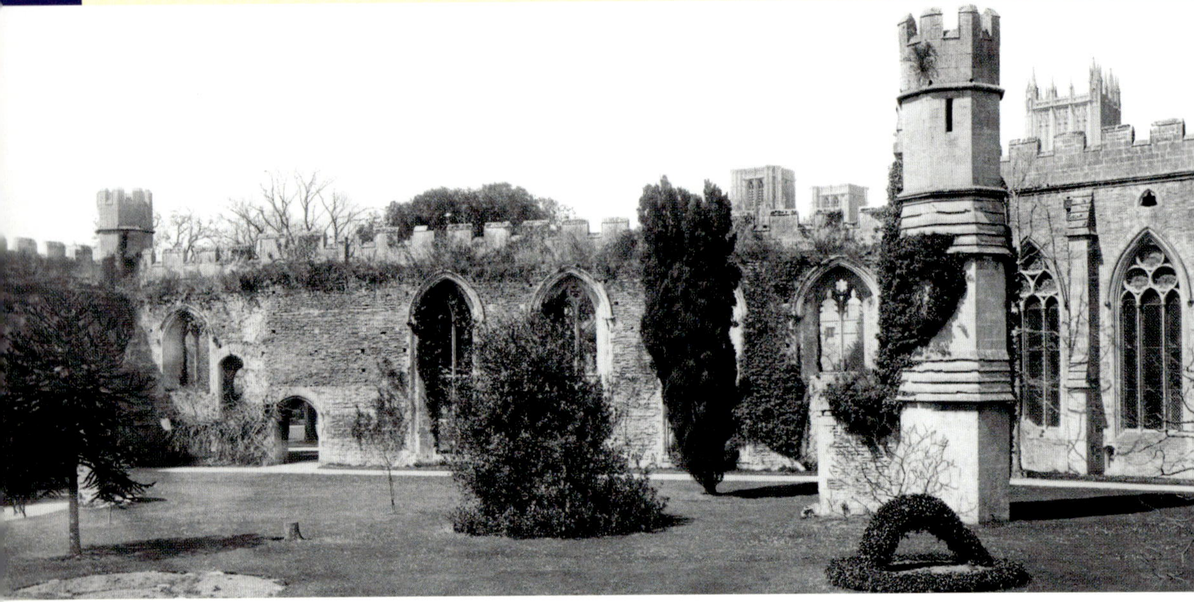

Set behind battlemented walls and surrounded by a moat fed by the resurgent waters, the palace was begun by Bishop Jocelin in the 13th century. Added to by his successors over the next two centuries, it served as the bishop's official residence. These ruins and other buildings still used today are set amid peaceful gardens, which are a haven from the city outside.

This classic view shows to good advantage Worcester Cathedral's splendid central tower and the west window (designed c1870 by Sir George Gilbert Scott). The cathedral was begun in 1084, but the exterior is largely the result of 13th- and 14th-century rebuilding and 19th-century restoration. The original tower collapsed in 1175, and its replacement was not completed until 1374.

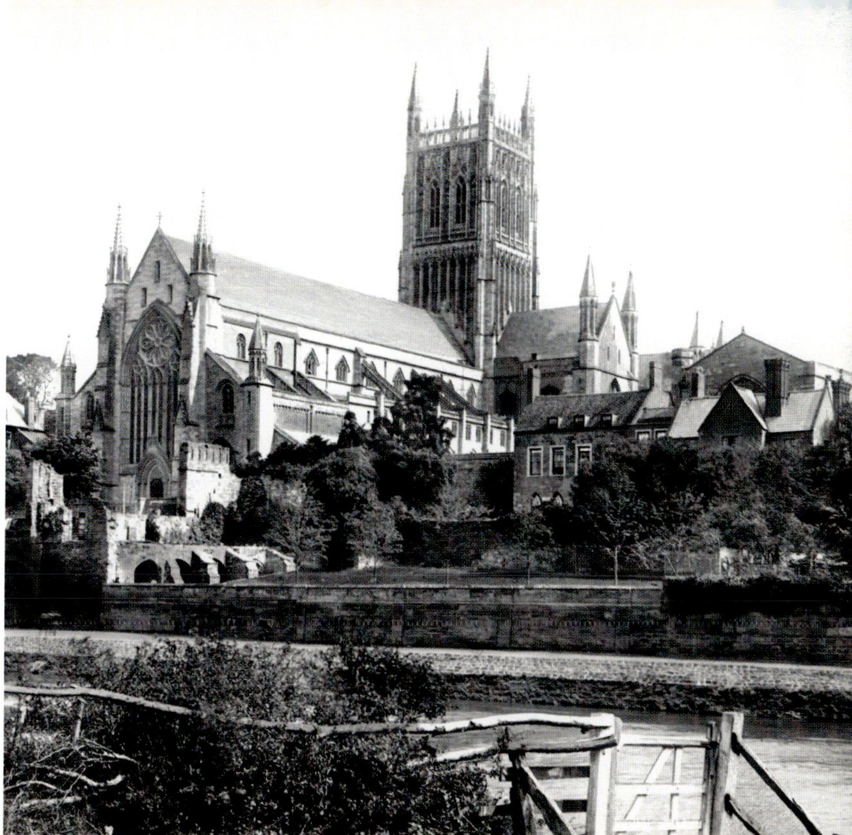

WORCESTER, THE CATHEDRAL, THE WEST FRONT 1891 29298

WINCHESTER, THE CATHEDRAL 1911 63722

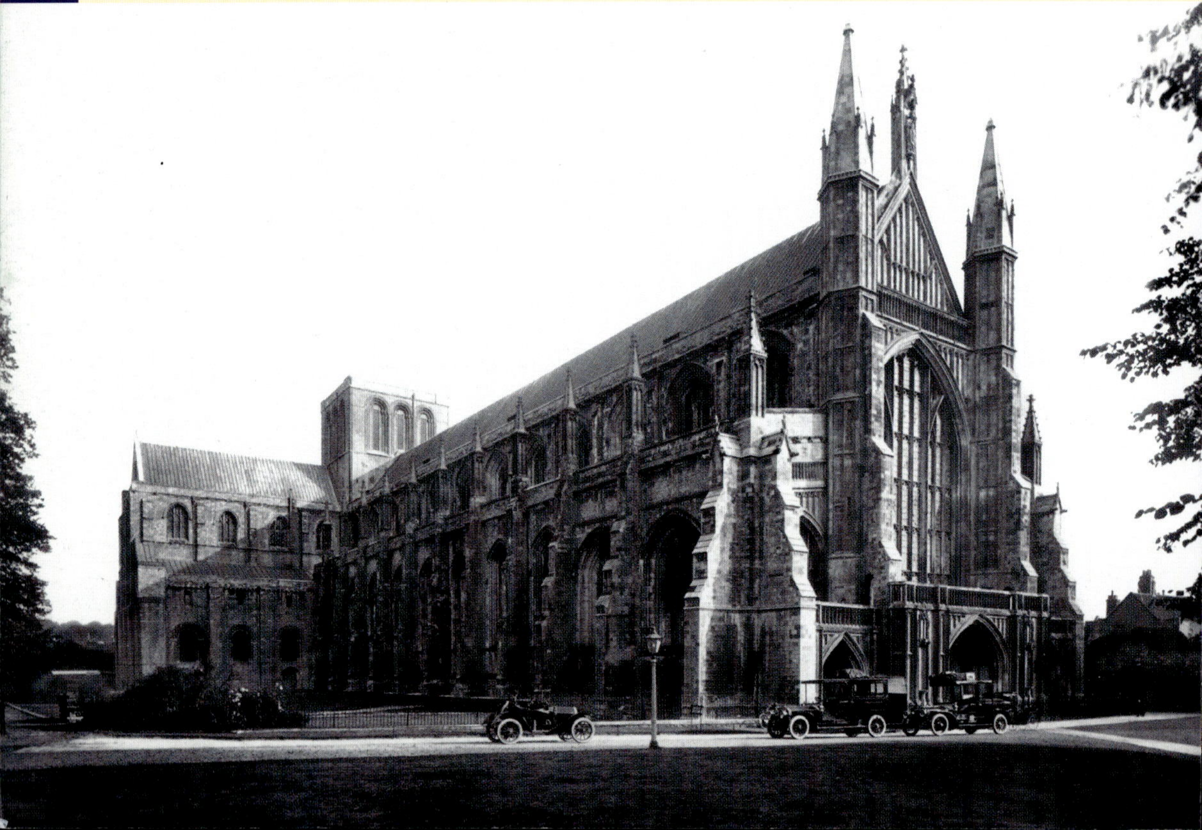

◄ *This splendid photograph gives us some idea of the immense length of Winchester Cathedral: at 556 feet, it is the longest Gothic church in Europe. A Saxon minster church was established here in 643, but it was the Norman bishop Walkelin who began the cathedral we see today. The cathedral stands on marshy ground, and the crypt often floods.*

► *This view of Worcester Cathedral was taken looking west along the length of the quire and nave to the great west window. The tomb in the foreground is that of King John (1167-1216), the first post-Conquest monarch to be buried in England; he lies at Worcester at his own request. In 1218 the remains of Worcester's two saints, Wulfstan and Oswald, were transferred from their original tombs to a shrine in the quire and King John was buried between them – they are represented by two small figures either side of his shoulders.*

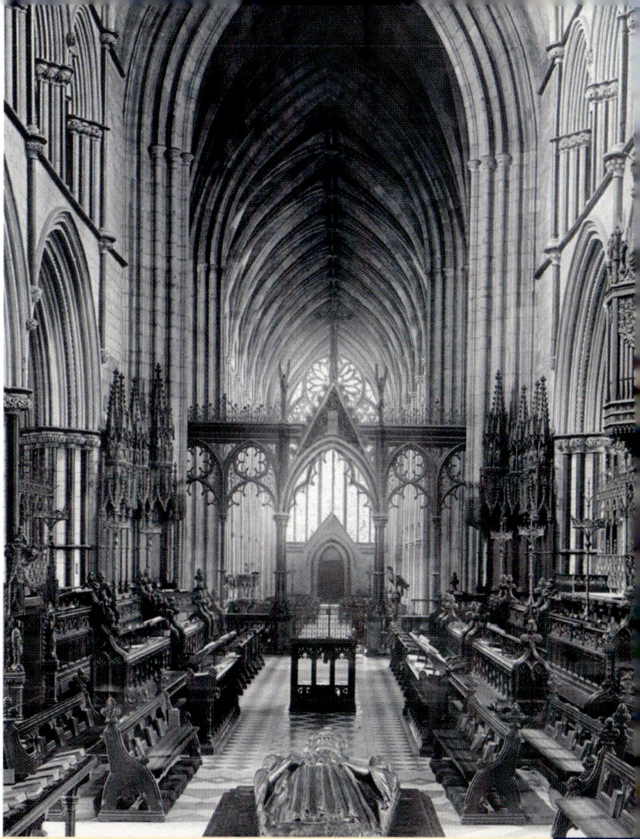

WORCESTER, THE CATHEDRAL QUIRE 1891 29313

WORCESTER, THE CATHEDRAL, THE CRYPT 1893 32101

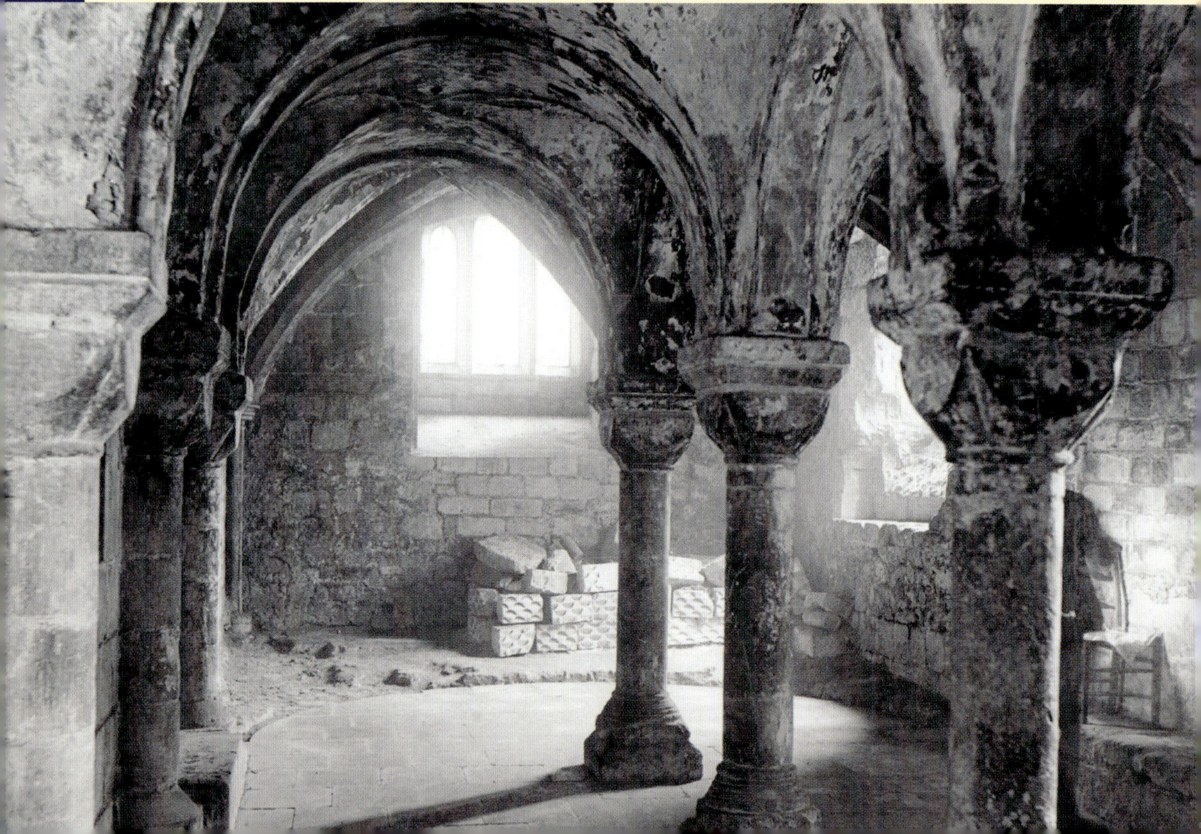

◄ *The earliest surviving structure in Worcester, and the largest Norman crypt in England, this is all that remains of St Wulfstan's cathedral of 1084. Built partly of reused masonry from St Oswald's Benedictine priory, it is very beautiful, with a forest of stone columns supporting a simple vaulted roof.*

► *Begun during the reign of King John and finally completed in 1472, York Minster stands on a site previously occupied by the Roman praetorium and by Saxon churches; the earliest of these was a small wattle oratory constructed for the baptism of Edwin, King of Northumbria, in 627. The minster is one of the largest cathedrals of England, and the western towers are 196 feet high.*

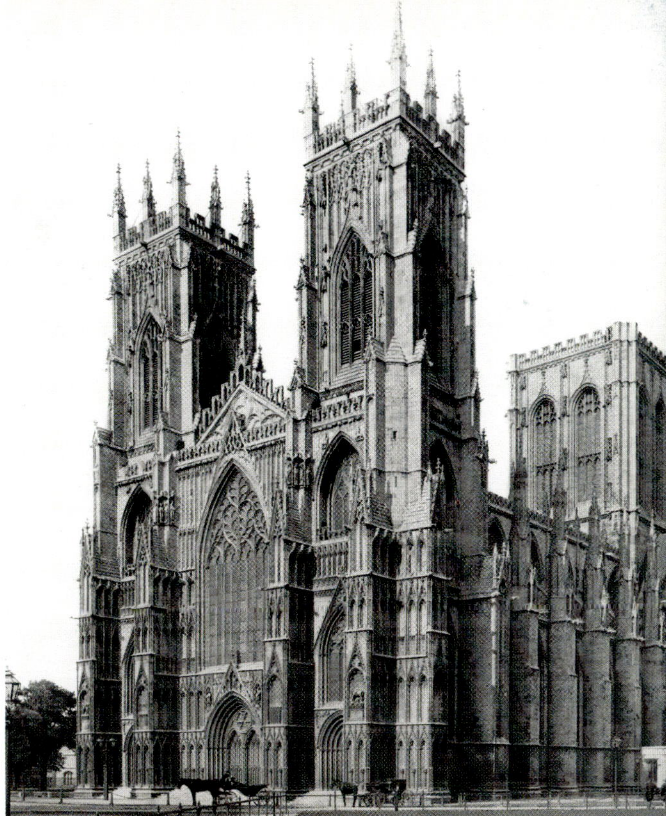

YORK, THE MINSTER, FROM THE SOUTH WEST c1880 12894

York Minster was undergoing repairs at the time of this photograph. Pollution, mainly from the smoke from the railway, did a lot of damage to both glass and stone. Also, between 1829 and 1984 there were three fires; the first was caused deliberately, the second by a careless workman, and the third by lightning. All three caused damage and loss, and much restoration has had to be carried out.

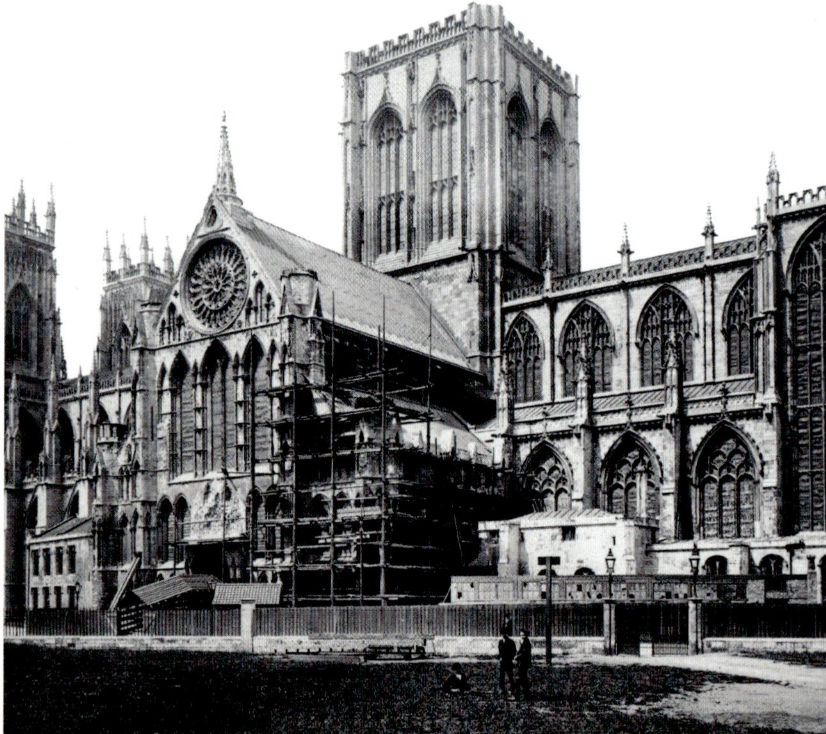

YORK, THE MINSTER c1890 Y12501

INDEX

FREE PRINT OF YOUR CHOICE

Choose any Frith photograph in this book.
Simply complete the Voucher opposite and return it with your remittance for £2.25 (to cover postage and handling) and we will print the photograph of your choice in SEPIA (size 11 x 8 inches) and supply it in a cream mount with a burgundy rule line (overall size 14 x 11 inches).

Please note: photographs with a reference number starting with a "Z" are not Frith photographs and cannot be supplied under this offer.
Offer valid for delivery to one UK address only.

PLUS: **Order additional Mounted Prints at HALF PRICE - £7.49 each** (normally £14.99)
If you would like to order more Frith prints from this book, possibly as gifts for friends and family, you can buy them at half price (with no additional postage and handling costs).

PLUS: **Have your Mounted Prints framed**
For an extra £14.95 per print you can have your mounted print(s) framed in an elegant polished wood and gilt moulding, overall size 16 x 13 inches (no additional postage and handling required).

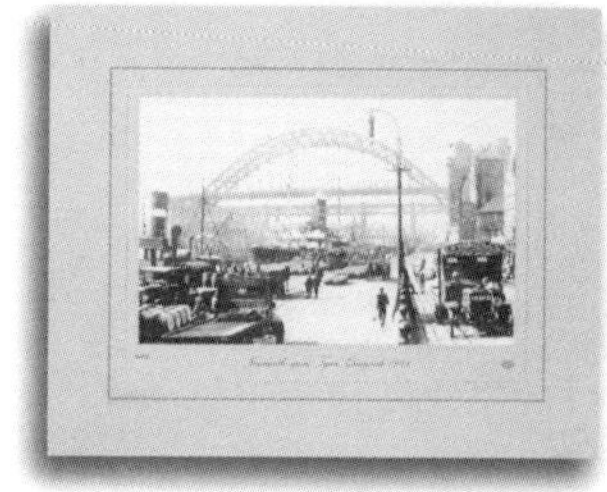

Mounted Print
Overall size 14 x 11 inches (355 x 280mm)

IMPORTANT!

These special prices are only available if you use this form to order. You must use the ORIGINAL VOUCHER (no copies permitted).

We can only despatch to one UK address. This offer cannot be combined with any other offer.

FRITH PRODUCTS AND SERVICES

All Frith photographs are available for you to buy as framed or mounted prints. From time to time, other illustrated items such as Address Books and Maps are also available. Already, almost 100,000 Frith archive photographs can be viewed and purchased on the internet through the Frith website.

For more detailed information on Frith companies and products, visit:

www.francisfrith.co.uk

For further information, contact:

The Francis Frith Collection, Frith's Barn,
Teffont, Salisbury SP3 5QP
Tel: +44 (0) 1722 716 376
Fax: +44 (0) 1722 716 881
Email: sales@francisfrith.co.uk

Send completed Voucher form to:

The Francis Frith Collection, Frith's Barn, Teffont, Salisbury, Wiltshire SP3 5QP England

If you need more space, please write your address on a separate sheet of paper.

Voucher

for FREE and Reduced Price Frith Prints

Do not photocopy this voucher. Only the original is valid, so please fill it in, cut it out and return it to us with your order.

	Picture ref no	Page number	Qty	Mounted @ £7.49	Framed + £14.95	Order Total £
1			1	Free of charge*	£	£
2				£7.49	£	£
3				£7.49	£	£
4				£7.49	£	£
5				£7.49	£	£
6				£7.49	£	£
				* Post & handling		£2.25
				Total Order Cost		£

Please allow 28 days for delivery. Offer available to one UK address only

Title of this book . . . .

I enclose a cheque / postal order for £ . . . .
payable to 'The Francis Frith Collection'

OR debit my Mastercard / Visa / Maestro card

Card Number

Issue No (Maestro only)   Valid from (Maestro)

Expires   Signature

Name Mr/Mrs/Ms ....

Address ....

....

....

....Postcode..............................

Daytime Tel No ....

E-mail ....

ISBN 1-84589-084-1

Valid to 31/12/08